Fr. Robert J Kus

FLOWERS IN THE WIND 4

MORE STORY~BASED HOMILIES FOR CYCLE A

RED LANTERN PRESS
WILMINGTON, NORTH CAROLINA

www.redlanternpress.com

Books by Red Lantern Press

Journals by Fr. Robert J. Kus

- *Dreams for the Vineyard: Journal of a Parish Priest* - 2002

- *For Where Your Treasure Is: Journal of a Parish Priest* – 2003

- *There Will Your Heart Be Also: Journal of a Parish Priest* – 2004

- *Field of Plenty: Journal of a Parish Priest* – 2005

- *Called to the Coast: Journal of a Parish Priest* – 2006

- *Then Along Came Marcelino: Journal of a Parish Priest* – 2007

- *Living the Dream: Journal of a Parish Priest* – 2008

- *A Hand to Honduras: Journal of a Parish Priest* - 2009

Homily Collections by Fr. Robert J. Kus

- *Flowers in the Wind 1 – Story-Based Homilies for Cycle B*

- *Flowers in the Wind 2 – Story-Based Homilies for Cycle C*

- *Flowers in the Wind 3 – Story-Based Homilies for Cycle A*

- *Flowers in the Wind 4 – More Story-Based Homilies for Cycle A*

ISBN: 1515157199
ISBN 13: 9781515157199

Dedication

To Padre Gerardo Alberto Vallecillo-Murcia

of the

Archdiocese of Tegucigalpa

Honduras

Acknowledgements

Many thanks go to Nolan Heath and Pat Marriott of the Basilica Shrine of St. Mary in Wilmington, N.C. who helped with the editing of these homilies.

Many thanks also go to the parishioners of both St. Catherine of Siena Parish in Wake Forest, N.C. and the Basilica Shrine of St. Mary for whom I originally created these homilies.

Table of Contents

Introduction

Introduction

The purpose of this book is to provide Catholic preachers a second complete collection of Sunday (& Christmas) homilies for Cycle A. Though it is designed specifically for Catholic priests and deacons, the homilies should prove useful for preachers in other mainstream Christian denominations as well.

Each homily starts with the Sunday of the Year being celebrated followed by the Scripture selection that is being discussed. This is followed by a story that appeals for people of all ages. Finally, each homily then discusses the concepts that can be gleaned from the Scripture and story and how we can apply them to our everyday lives.

Each homily takes less than eight minutes. This is especially important for preachers who are in parishes that have Masses every 90 minutes and have to get parking lots filled and emptied in a limited amount of time.

The homilies were created while I was pastor of parishes with large concentrations of children. I'm happy to say the stories make the homilies vibrant and interesting, and families love talking about the stories during the week.

Preachers may take the homilies whole, or they may tweak them to fit their specific needs.

Every effort has been made to credit the authors of each story. In the event that this was not possible, the story sources are listed as being written by "Anonymous."

Part One

ADVENT &
CHRISTMAS SEASONS

Chapter 1

1st Sunday of Advent - A
Cherokee Tree Story

Scripture:

- Isaiah 2: 1-5
- Psalm 122: 1-2, 3-4ab, 4cd-5, 6-7, 8-9
- Romans 13: 11-14
- Matthew 24: 37-44

Today we begin the Season of Advent, the beginning of a brand new Church Year, Year A. During this Church Year, most of the Gospel selections will be from the Gospel of Matthew.

Advent, like all seasons of the Church Year, is joyful in nature. Specifically, Advent is known as the "season of joyful expectation." What we are waiting for is the coming of Jesus Christ. During the first two weeks of Advent, we focus on the Second Coming of Jesus at the end of time, while in the second two weeks of Advent, we focus on the coming of Jesus as the Christ Child on Christmas.

Whether we are focusing on Jesus coming at the end of time or at Christmas, we are called during Advent to be waiting and watching. "Waiting" does mean simply sitting around twiddling our thumbs, and "watching" does not mean standing around looking up at the sky. Rather, "waiting and watching" means that we are to live our lives in such a way that we are always ready for the coming of the Lord.

The importance of watching is seen in this wonderful old Cherokee story about why some trees stay green all through the winter months.

When the Great Spirit created the plants and trees of the world, he decided to give each species a special gift. But first, the Great Spirit decided to have a contest to see what kind of gift would be most appropriate for each species.

The Great Spirit told all the trees and plants that he wanted them to stay awake and keep watch over all the Earth for seven days and nights. The plant kingdom was thrilled to be so honored. Therefore, filled with excitement, none of them found it difficult to stay away the first night. The second night, however, was not so easy, and some members of the plant kingdom fell asleep. The same thing happened on each of the following nights.

When the seventh night came, the only members of the plant kingdom still awake were the pine, cedar, laurel, fir, holly, and spruce. The Great Spirit was very impressed with these species that remained alert through the whole week. "Therefore," said the Great Spirit, "I shall give you the gift of forever staying green. From now on, even in the dead of winter, you shall be green and shall be the guardians of the forest. All the other trees and plants shall lose their leaves in winter and fall asleep, but you shall always be awake."

This beautiful Cherokee Indian tale is a great Advent story, for Advent is noted for waiting and watching. In spiritual literature, "staying awake" is a code word for remaining tuned in to God regardless of what is going on in our lives. During wakes and funerals, for example, we are reminded of this very thing, that we should always live our lives in readiness for the Lord because we never know when He will come for us.

But how are we supposed to stay ready for the Lord? We know that one day the Lord will knock on our door, take us by the hand, and say, "Come with me. My Father has your place all ready for you." And he will lead us into eternity. But we don't know if this will happen in the next thirty minutes, thirty days, or thirty years. We only know that at an unknown time, our time on Earth will end.

I believe there are three solid ways to be ready for the Lord.

First, we stay in contact with the Lord through prayer. Prayer is nothing more than chatting with the Lord. I recommend that we not let our feet touch the floor in the morning without first praying. That prayer could be something very simple such as, "Thanks for the night of sleep, Lord. Be with me through the day."

All through the day, we should keep on praying. We can pray while brushing our teeth, working on our computer, changing a diaper, washing dishes, driving a car, or whatever. Now many people think prayer has to be very complicated and long. That is false. Two of my favorite prayers are: "Help!" and "Thanks!" Both of those prayers put together only took about one second. Therefore, never say you are "too busy" to pray; that is ridiculous. At the end of the day, thank God for all the blessings you receive and make a promise to do better tomorrow.

Second, we stay ready for the Lord when we live our vocations to the best of our ability. That means getting into life with full gusto. It means making the most of our time, talent, and treasure. It means that if God has called you to be a mother, be the best mother you can possibly be...or the best student or best musician or best whatever.

And finally, we remain ready for the Lord when we follow the triple love commandment of Jesus Christ—to love God, to love our neighbor, and to love ourselves. Needless to say, we have hundreds of opportunities to show our love for God by serving those in need all around us. It means remembering that Jesus lives in all people, so how we treat another is how

5

we treat Christ. It also means that we treat our own selves with respect as children of God by caring for our physical, mental and spiritual life.

As we continue our life journeys this week, it would be a good idea to take stock of our own lives. Are we ready for the Lord by keeping in touch with him, living our vocations as best we can, and loving God, others, and self?

And that is the good news I have for you on this First Sunday of Advent.

Story source: "Why Some Trees Are Evergreen," in William J. Bausch (Ed.), *A World of Stories for Preachers and Teachers,* 1998, #87, pp. 235-236.

Chapter 2

2nd Sunday of Advent - A
Desiderata

Scripture:

- Isaiah 11: 1-10
- Psalm 72: 1-2, 7-8, 12-13, 17
- Romans 15: 4-9
- Matthew 3: 1-12

As we gather to celebrate the Eucharist today on this Second Sunday of Advent, we encounter the theme of peace, which, in Biblical context, means harmony.

During Advent, the readings all have to do with what it will be like when the Messiah comes. Isaiah, for example, sees nothing but harmony, a world where even natural enemies such as the wolf and the lamb will be friends. Paul echoes this call for peace when he tells his followers to be at peace with one another. And in the Gospel reading of today, we hear John the Baptizer telling the Pharisees and Sadducees that it is not enough to simply celebrate rituals or be descendants of Abraham. Rather, John insists that they live their lives in such a way that they will actually produce "good fruit."

Unfortunately for us in twenty-first century United States, Advent is almost the opposite of what the liturgical season intends. Instead of being a peaceful time, it often leads us to be frantic in preparing for Christmas, going to endless parties and plays and concerts, shopping for presents, sending out cards, and in the process, becoming frazzled and stressed out. By the time Christmas comes, many of us are exhausted.

There is hope, however. We can slow down. We can "get a grip" on the meaning of Advent. We can deliberately take some time to spend in solitude with God.

One of the most beautiful pieces of writing that I know of that reflects the basic nature of both Advent and of life in general, was written by Max Ehrmann in Indiana in 1927. It is called *Desiderata*, meaning "Things to be desired," and it goes like this:

> *Go placidly amid the noise and haste,*
> *and remember what peace there may be in silence.*
>
> *As far as possible without surrender*
> *be on good terms with all persons.*
> *Speak your truth quietly and clearly;*
> *and listen to others,*
> *even the dull and the ignorant;*
> *they too have their story.*

DESIDERATA

Avoid loud and aggressive persons,
they are vexatious to the spirit.

If you compare yourself with others,
you may become vain and bitter;
for always there will be greater and lesser persons than yourself.

Enjoy your achievements as well as your plans.
Keep interested in your own career, however humble;
it is a real possession in the changing fortunes of time.
Exercise caution in your business affairs;
for the world is full of trickery.
But let this not blind you to what virtue there is;
many persons strive for high ideals;
and everywhere life is full of heroism.

Be yourself.
Especially, do not feign affection.
Neither be cynical about love;
for in the face of all aridity and disenchantment
it is as perennial as the grass.

Take kindly the counsel of the years,
gracefully surrendering the things of youth.
Nurture strength of spirit to shield you in sudden misfortune.

But do not distress yourself with dark imaginings.
Many fears are born of fatigue and loneliness.

Beyond a wholesome discipline,
be gentle with yourself.
You are a child of the universe,
no less than the trees and the stars;
you have a right to be here.
And whether or not it is clear to you,
no doubt the universe is unfolding as it should.

Therefore be at peace with God,
whatever you conceive Him to be,
and whatever your labors and aspirations,
in the noisy confusion of life keep peace with your soul.

With all its sham, drudgery, and broken dreams,
it is still a beautiful world.
Be cheerful.
Strive to be happy.

What incredible wisdom and joy and hope this piece of writing contains.

As we continue our life journeys this week, how do we reflect the call for simplicity and peacefulness of this Advent season? What can we do to become more peaceful in our own lives?

And that is the good news I have for you on this Second Sunday of Advent.

Chapter 3

3rd Sunday of Advent - A
Our Lady of Guadalupe

Scripture:

- Isaiah 35: 1-6a, 10
- Psalm 146: 6c-7, 8-9a, 9bc-10
- James 5: 7-10
- Matthew 11: 2-11

The Third Sunday of Advent is called Gaudete Sunday, the Sunday of Joy. In the reading from the Prophet Isaiah, we hear how wonderful it will be when the Messiah comes. Specifically, Isaiah dreamt of a Messiah who will heal those who are feeble and lame and blind. He will strengthen hearts that are afraid and save those who are lost. In the Gospel reading from Matthew, we hear that Jesus, the Messiah, actually is doing what Isaiah prophesized: he is cleansing lepers, giving sight to the blind, giving hearing to the deaf, and even raising the dead. As for the poor, he is proclaiming good news to them.

It is little wonder, then, that this Sunday is called Gaudete Sunday, for it is indeed filled with joyful news.

But the good news of Biblical times continues through the centuries. Today, for example, we encounter one of the most powerful and exciting stories of the Advent Season, the story of our Lady of Guadalupe.

The story begins in Mexico on December 9, 1531. On this day, a fifty-seven year old Chichimeca Indian by the name of "The Eagle Who Talks" in his language, but today called Juan Diego, was walking fifteen miles to daily Mass. As Juan Diego was passing Tepeyac Hill near what is now Mexico City, he saw a glowing cloud encircled by a rainbow. He also heard music. When he looked up, he was amazed to see a beautiful young woman dressed like an Aztec princess.

Although the Virgin Mary is believed to have appeared at other ages and in other places, this apparition was unusual. This apparition had the beautiful skin color of a *mestizo* (a person of Spanish and native heritage) and spoke Nahuatl, the native language spoken by Juan Diego. The symbolism of the skin color and language was powerful, for the apparition appeared to be one of the poor of society instead of one of the rich and powerful.

The woman told Juan Diego that she was the Virgin Mary and that she wanted a church to be built on that very site so that "...in it, I can be present and give my love, compassion, help, and defense, for I am your most devoted mother...to hear your laments and to remedy all your miseries, pains, and sufferings."

Juan Diego immediately went to visit the bishop. The bishop spoke only Spanish, and Juan Diego spoke only Nahuatl, but through translators, the bishop said he needed a sign. Therefore, Juan Diego went to search for some sign. But on his way, he discovered that his uncle, Juan Bernardino, was dying. Therefore, he immediately went searching for a priest. But while Juan Diego was on his way to get a priest to anoint his uncle, the Virgin Mary appeared to him once again and told him that his uncle was cured.

The Virgin Mary then told Juan Diego to go onto the top of Tepeyac Hill to gather Castilian roses that were growing in frozen soil and take them to the bishop. Juan Diego obeyed and gathered many of these roses, a kind that did not grow in Mexico, and put them in his cloak.

Juan Diego told the bishop what had happened and opened his cloak to show him the mystical roses. As the flowers fell to the floor, the bishop was astonished to see on Juan Diego's cloak the image of the Virgin Mary. Today, this image is known as that of Our Lady of Guadalupe.

Soon after this miracle, the bishop built a church on that spot. Hundreds of thousands of people were converted there to Catholic Christianity.

In 1945, Pope Pius XII proclaimed Our Lady of Guadalupe to be "The Queen of Mexico and Empress of the Americas." It is thus that the picture of Our Lady of Guadalupe, Patron Saint of the Americas, is seen in many Catholic churches in North, Central, and South American nations.

Juan Diego, the simple and humble Indian man, lived until he was seventy-four years old. For the remainder of his life, he is said to have devoted his life to humbly serving the pilgrims who came to visit the cloak on which the Virgin of Guadalupe was imprinted. Pope John Paul II proclaimed him a saint in 2002. At his canonization, John Paul praised Juan Diego as a model of simplicity and humility for all people.

The story of Our Lady of Guadalupe is indeed a magnificent one, a perfect story for Gaudete Sunday in particular. This story highlights God's continual watching over his creation throughout the ages.

The story of Our Lady of Guadalupe is especially important today, when greed and nationalism and racism infect the hearts and minds of so many people, even Catholic Christians who should know better. The story of Our Lady of Guadalupe serves as a reminder of the commitment of the Catholic Church throughout the world to what the Church Fathers at the Second Vatican Council called "the preferential option for the poor." In other words, Catholic Christians must always and everywhere put the

<u>needs</u> of the poor ahead of the <u>desires</u> of the rich. For if we do not do that, we are not worthy to be called Catholic Christians.

As we continue our life journey this week, it would be a good idea to reflect on the story of Our Lady of Guadalupe. How do we put the needs of the poor before our own desires?

And that is the good news I have for you on this Third Sunday of Advent, Gaudete Sunday.

<u>Story source:</u> Richard McBrien (Ed.), *The Harpercollins Encyclopedia of Catholicism*, 1995, pp. 594-596.

Chapter 4

4th Sunday of Advent - A
Vocational Messages

Scripture:

- Isaiah 7: 10-14
- Psalm 24: 1-2, 3-4ab, 5-6
- Romans 1: 1-7
- Matthew 1: 18-24

Today as we gather to celebrate the Eucharist on this Fourth Sunday of Advent, we hear the story of how Joseph came to accept Mary as his wife.

We hear that when Joseph learned that his wife Mary was pregnant, they had not yet been together. Therefore, he thought it would be wise to quietly divorce Mary so that she would not be exposed to shame. God, however, sent an angel to Joseph in a dream. The angel told Joseph that Mary had become pregnant by the Holy Spirit, that she would bear a son who was to be named Jesus, and that the son would grow up to "save his people." The angel also told Joseph not to be afraid to take Mary into his home as his wife. Joseph, being a holy man, followed God's will.

Now this is a wonderful story, for sure. However, when we hear such stories, we may say to ourselves, "Well, if God sent an angel to me to tell me what I should do, I'd be happy to do it. Unfortunately, God never sends me an angel, so I don't know what I am supposed to do with my life. Should I take the job offer in New Mexico? Should I buy a house or rent a house? What should I major in at college? I wish I could have an angel tell me these things!"

Well, believe it or not, God is still sending us messengers to guide us on our life journeys. True, they are not the winged creatures you see in paintings. Rather, the messages God sends often come through other human beings. Although there are many ways God does this, today I will talk about just three of the ways God guides us in making decisions about our lives.

First, God communicates through writers and their works. An excellent example of a man whose life was changed by writing was Ignatius of Loyola.

Young Ignatius was a Spanish soldier who had great dreams of being a military hero. One day, however, a cannon ball shattered his leg. As a result, he was taken to a castle to begin the long process of recovery. He wanted some romance novels to read, but the castle didn't have any of those on hand. What they did have, however, were books on the life of Christ and the lives of the saints. Ignatius, therefore, settled for them.

God changed Ignatius through this literature. Now, instead of dreaming of being a great military knight, Ignatius decided to devote his life to becoming a great saint. Through much prayer and meditation, along with intense mental and spiritual suffering, he began to develop himself spiritually. Soon he attracted like-minded men around him, and together they formed a religious community called the Society of Jesus. During his life, Ignatius and his fellow Jesuits founded hospitals, schools, and orphanages, and they took the faith throughout the world as missionaries. And in time, Ignatius too became a Catholic writer whose works have influenced millions of people through the centuries.

A second way God leads us on our vocational journey is through family members. A good example of this is seen in the life of Blessed Louis Martin, father of St. Therese of Lisieux, the "Little Flower."

Louis was a Frenchman who loved his family very much and who was a very pious Catholic man. Louis and his wife Zelie had nine children, four of whom died in infancy. The other five children, all girls, grew up to become nuns.

When Therese was a little girl, her father would take her on walks and talk about the wonders of nature. From her father, she fell in love with God's awesome creation, especially trees and flowers and the other elements of nature. But Louis also helped the girls learn about prayer, and the love of God and God's Church. But the greatest gift Louis gave to the Church was nurturing the religious vocations of his daughters. In her writings, St. Therese talks about how her father would take her as a little girl to the local convent of the Discalced Carmelite nuns. He would tell her that behind those walls lived very holy people. From these conversations, Therese developed a great desire to become a Discalced Carmelite nun. She became not only such a nun, but she became a saint in the process. Both of her parents, Louis and Zelie Martin, were declared "Blessed" in 2008.

A third way that God can guide us on our life journey is through what I call the "closed door syndrome." God does this by closing doors that he does not want us to enter. When this happens, we are often sad and discouraged. The better way to react to closed doors is to say, "God closed this door because he has something so much better in mind for me!" If you live long enough, you will see this is indeed true over, and over, and over again!

A great example of the closed-door syndrome is seen in the life of St. Benedict Joseph Labré. From the time he was a little boy, he desperately wanted to become a priest. His uncle, who was a parish priest, educated him and encouraged him. Unfortunately, however, every religious Order that Benedict tried to enter rejected him.

Benedict, when he was twenty-two years old, accepted the fact that God did not want him to become a priest. Therefore, he became a lay brother and a tramp, walking around Europe as a simple homeless man, visiting churches, and praying. In 1883, he was declared a Saint of the Catholic Church and declared the Patron Saint of tramps and homeless people!

So, God still sends messengers to us as he did to Joseph centuries ago. Today we saw just three ways he communicates to us: through writers, through family members, and through closed doors. How is God communicating to you today?

And that is the good news I have for you on this Fourth Sunday of Advent.

Chapter 5

Christmas- A
The Russian Prince

Scripture – [Midnight]:

- Isaiah 9: 1-6
- Psalm 96: 1-2a, 2b-3, 11-12, 13
- Titus 2: 11-14
- Luke 2: 1-14

On behalf of the staff, faculty, and all the ministers of our parish, I wish you and those you love a very Merry Christmas!

We come today to celebrate the birth of the Messiah, the Savior who was promised by God to the Hebrew people many centuries ago.

The Hebrew people did not know exactly what kind of Messiah to expect, but their writings indicate that they thought he would be a great king reigning in splendor. When he came, they imagined, everything would be wonderful. Peace would flow like a river, and harmony would rule over all of nature. In short, it would be heaven on Earth.

Little did they expect that the Messiah would be a humble child born in a manger to a simple couple who came from a small town. But, indeed, that is what happened. God knew that the people often had trouble following his own laws, so God thought that if he were to become human and dwell among humanity, perhaps the people would pay more attention. So, that is how Jesus, one hundred percent human and one hundred percent divine, came to be born in Bethlehem to Mary and her husband Joseph.

And sure enough, Jesus did have an impact on the people, growing up to be a miracle worker and storyteller and champion of the poor and downtrodden of society and a healer of the sick in mind and body and spirit. Yes, indeed, living among the people was quite an amazing stroke of divine genius.

That is similar to what happened to a young prince who lived in medieval Russia. As the story goes, there was once a handsome young prince named Alexis who lived in a magnificent palace. Unfortunately, all around the palace were filthy hovels where poor peasants lived.

When Prince Alexis saw how miserably the people lived, his heart was touched to the core. He was moved with compassion for the poor people, and he was determined to make their lives easier. Therefore, he regularly left the castle to visit them. But as he moved in and out of his castle, he had no point of contact with the people. Oh, sure, the people were very respectful towards him. In fact, they practically worshiped him. But they never actually warmed up to him, and he could never win their confidence or affection. They treated him as someone totally out of their league. Therefore, he would end his trips into the poor kingdom sad and disappointed.

Then one day, a very different kind of man entered the lives of the people. He was a rough-and-ready young doctor who wanted to devote his life to serving the poor. To begin, he rented a dirty, rundown shack in one of the back streets of the city. To fit in with the people, he wore the same kind of clothes they wore, old and tattered, and he ate only the plainest food, often not even knowing where the next meal was coming from.

The young doctor made very little money off his medical practice because he was forever treating people for free and giving away medicines. And, he would chat with the people, listening to their problems. He would laugh at the children's jokes. He would cry with families when they had to bury a loved one. Before long, the young doctor had won the respect and affection of all the people in a way that Prince Alexis had never been able to do. The doctor was, after all, one of them. And little by little, he transformed the whole spirit of the city, settling quarrels, helping people to live decent lives, and getting enemies to become friends.

Nobody in the kingdom ever guessed that this young doctor was actually Prince Alexis in disguise. He had left his magnificent palace to come down and dwell among the people and become one of them. As a result, the young prince was able to accomplish as a commoner what, as a lofty prince, he was never able to do.

And that, of course, is just what God the Son did for us. He left heaven to come and dwell among us. He played in the dusty streets of his town with the other boys. He learned to be a carpenter from his foster-father, Joseph. He hung around with those whom religious leaders condemned. He went sailing with fishermen, rugged men whom he made his apostles. And he taught the people how to love one another.

Two thousand years have gone by since Jesus walked among us as a child, a youth, and a young man. But his message of love has been passed down through the ages to us today. And like people all over the world, we come to church to celebrate his birth.

We come to church with all our problems and joys. Some come here today filled with anxiety over bills and a lack of job. Others are filled with worries about their adult children who seem to have gone astray. Others worry about the future.

But all of us, no matter what our life circumstances, should also come to the Christ Child with dreams, for Christmas is for dreamers. Christmas is a time to dream of a brighter future. It is a time to dream of becoming holier, bathing in the light of Christ. It is a time to dream of living our lives in a more generous and joyful and love-centered way. It is a time to dream of becoming the Christians we are called to be.

Whatever your Christmas dreams are, I pray that they will come true! And that is the good news I have for you on this Christmas.

Story source: "The Russian Prince" story is in Anthony Castle's *A Treasury of Quips, Quotes, & Anecdotes for Preachers & Teachers,* 1998, pp. 218-219.

Chapter 6

Holy Family - A
Carving a Wooden Bowl

Scripture]:

- Sirach 3: 2-6, 12-14
- Psalm 128: 1-2, 3, 4-5
- Colossians 3: 12-21
- Matthew 2: 13-15, 19-23

Today the Catholic Church celebrates the Feast of the Holy Family of Jesus, Mary, and Joseph.

Appropriately, all of the Scripture readings of the day reflect the theme of "family." In the Gospel reading, for example, we hear about how the Holy Family had to flee to Egypt to escape the genocide of male children that King Herod was planning. In the Old Testament reading from Sirach, we hear how we are to honor our parents. And in St. Paul's Letter to the Colossians, we are reminded to treat everyone as family.

Although there are many aspects of family to explore, today I will focus on how we are to treat the elderly among us. Though I think all of us want to be kind and considerate towards the elderly members of our families, sometimes we need a reminder. That is exactly what the young parents in the following story learned the hard way.

There was once young couple named Thomas and Mary who had a four-year old son named Philip. They were a very happy family and had a clean and cozy home. One day, Thomas decided that his father, Philip's grandfather, was too frail to be living by himself. Therefore, the young family invited the grandfather into their home to live.

Soon, however, problems arose. Though the grandfather was a perfect gentleman and did his best, he was old and frail, didn't see well, and his hands shook so much at times that he broke dishes and cups when he ate, and often spilled milk and soup when he was eating.

Mary became exasperated at Grandfather when he spilled milk or dropped food or broke a dish or dropped his fork. She would say unkind things to him when he had an accident at the table. Thomas agreed. The mess Grandfather always made at the table irritated him too. Therefore, Thomas put a card table in the corner of the kitchen. Then he told Grandfather that that is where he would be eating from now on. Further, to prevent his father from breaking any more dishes, Thomas gave him a wooden bowl to eat from.

Each meal from then on, Grandfather sat at the little card table alone while the rest of the family sat at the big table enjoying each other's company and conversation. Sometimes the family would glance in Grandfather's direction, and they would see a tear in his eye as he did his best to eat. Nevertheless, every time Grandfather dropped his fork, spilled milk, or dropped food, Mary or Thomas would have nothing but harsh words for him. Four-year old Philip watched all of this in silence.

Then one evening before dinner, Thomas saw his little son sitting on the kitchen floor with some scraps of wood. Thomas asked his son, "Philip, what are you doing?"

The little boy replied, "Oh, I'm making a wooden bowl for you and Mama to eat your food out of when I grow up and you're old like Grandpa."

These words pierced the hearts of Thomas and Mary. They were speechless, and tears began to roll down their cheeks. Though they were speechless, they both knew what they had to do.

That evening, they got rid of the card table in the corner and gently guided Grandfather back to the family table. For the remainder of his life, Grandfather ate all of his meals with his family, and for some reason, Thomas and Mary never found his awkward eating habits troublesome.

This is indeed a powerful story. And from this story and that of the Scripture selections on this Feast of the Holy Family, we can learn several things. Here are just three.

First, we are to treat elderly members of our families with respect. That is part of the commandment to honor our fathers and our mothers.

Unfortunately, however, in the United States many elderly people are not respected and not treated with dignity. The National Center on Elder Abuse estimated that the elderly often experience physical abuse, emotional or psychological abuse, verbal abuse and threats, financial abuse, sexual abuse, exploitation, and neglect or abandonment.

Second, actions speak louder than words. This is seen so clearly in the story of the little boy and the wooden bowl he was making for his parents. Children so easily grasp their parents' truths.

Third, because we all share the same Father in heaven, every human being on the planet is our brother or sister. Therefore, we are to treat all people with dignity and respect by virtue of their humanity. That is the foundation of all Jesus' teaching.

As we continue our life journeys this week, it would be a good idea to take stock in our own lives of how we are treating the elderly.

And that is the good news I have for you on this Feast of the Holy Family.

Story source: "Carving a Wooden Bowl." In www.Snopes.Com: Rumor Has It. Based on the fables of Leo Tolstoy.

Chapter 7

Epiphany - A
The Hat in Church

Scripture:

- Isaiah 60: 1-6
- Psalm 72: 1-2, 7-8, 10-11, 12-13
- Ephesians 3: 2-3a, 5-6
- Matthew 2: 1-12

Today we celebrate the Feast of the Epiphany, also known as the Feast of the Three Kings or "Little Christmas." This is a very ancient feast, celebrated in the Church even longer than Christmas itself. In the Western branch of the Catholic Church, to which we belong, this feast celebrates the showing of Jesus to the magi or wise men from the East who brought gifts to Jesus.

Because the gifts brought by the magi were gold, frankincense, and myrrh, the Church has held that each symbolizes some aspect of Jesus. The gold celebrates his kingship; the frankincense symbolizes his divinity; and the sweet-smelling myrrh symbolizes his eventual crucifixion, as myrrh was the scented oil used on dead bodies in those days.

For us as Catholic Christians, the most important thing about this feast is not gift giving. Rather, it is that Jesus came for all people, not just for the Hebrews. For those of us living the twenty-first century, this is not news. But for the people in the early Church, that was amazing news indeed.

Because Jesus is for all people, as Catholic Christians we are to not only proclaim the good news of Jesus Christ to everyone on Earth, but we are to welcome the stranger. This is a very important concept to remember, especially this week as Catholic Christians in the United States celebrate National Migration Week.

Sometimes, however, we become lax in this regard. Instead of practicing "inclusion" we fall into "exclusion." We become insular in our own little groups within our parish. We forget that we are part of something much bigger, namely the Kingdom of God.

When we do forget to welcome the stranger, we sometimes need a reminder. That is what the priest and congregation of one church learned the hard way.

One day, at a very crowded church service, a man entered the church. As you know, in Catholic Churches, men and boys are expected to take off their hats as a sign of respect for the Lord. This man, however, refused to remove his hat even when the ushers asked him to do so. Some of the people of the assembly also asked him to remove his hat, but he still obstinately refused to do so.

The priest noticed the man, and was not very happy that the man spent the whole Mass with a hat on. Therefore, after the Mass was over and the priest was greeting the people, he stopped the man as he came out of church. He told the man that he was very happy to welcome him into the community, but that in the church, men and boys were not supposed to wear hats. The priest then said, "I hope you will conform to that custom in the future."

The man replied, "Thank you. And thank you for taking time to talk to me. I am very happy that you have invited me to join your parish. In fact, I joined it three years ago and have been coming regularly ever since. Today, however, is the first time anyone paid attention to me. After being ignored for three years by you and the members of the church, I decided today to keep my hat on so that others would maybe talk to me. And it worked. I had the pleasure of talking to the ushers. And now I am having a conversation with you, though you always seemed too busy to talk with me before."

Needless to say, the priest and the church members who overheard the conversation were amazed. And they were also very ashamed. Imagine, they thought, that a man could be coming regularly to our church for three years and not be welcomed by others. Soon, they began to change as a result of the "man with the hat."

Now in this story, I don't think that the priest or other members of the congregation were bad people. I doubt very seriously that they had deliberately ignored this man. Rather, they probably were like most of us, not paying attention at times to those around us.

Many people come to church each week filled with problems. Maybe they are battling a disease. Perhaps they can't pay their bills. Maybe they are so in love with their partner next to them that they can't see anyone else. Others may be in a deep depression, while others may be so worried about their children that they can't focus on others. There are even some who do not understand the real presence of Jesus Christ in the assembly, and therefore do not treat the people around them as the Body of Christ.

Finally, there are some people who deliberately ignore certain people in the congregation and deliberately snub them or give them dirty looks. Perhaps they don't like the looks of another person, the person with a nose ring or pink hair. Maybe they judge others in the congregation as morally inferior to themselves. Perhaps they are against people who speak a different language than they do, or who have a different skin color.

The reasons we do not welcome others are legion. The important thing is to remember that when we assemble to celebrate the Eucharist, Jesus Christ is really present in four ways: in the assembly; in the presider; in the proclaimed Scripture; and, after the Consecration, in the elements of bread and wine.

As we continue our life journeys this week, it would be a good idea to reflect on how we welcome the stranger among us when we come to Mass.

And that is the good news I have for you on this Feast of the Epiphany.

Story source: Anonymous, "On hospitality," in Brian Cavanaugh's *The Sower's Seeds,* 1990, #85, pp. 68-69.

Chapter 8

Baptism of the Lord Jesus - A
George Washington Carver

Scripture:

- Isaiah 42: 1-4, 6-7
- Psalm 29: 1a & 2, 3ac-4, 3b & 9b-10
- Acts of the Apostles 10: 34-38
- Matthew 3: 13-17

Today as we gather to celebrate the Eucharist, we hear the story of Jesus' baptism in the Jordan River by his cousin, John the Baptist.

John was very reluctant to baptize Jesus, for he felt that if anyone should be the baptizer, it should be Jesus. But Jesus asked John to humor him and baptize him anyway.

In Jesus' time, it was customary for Jews to baptize gentiles—non-Jews—who were converting to Judaism. And at the time of Jesus, it was just becoming fashionable for Jewish people themselves to become baptized as a sign of repentance. Needless to say, neither of these reasons fitted Jesus. First, he was already a Jewish man, not a convert. Second, he had nothing of which to repent.

So why did Jesus get baptized? Here are just three reasons.

First, by his baptism, Jesus cast his lot with humanity. Though he was fully divine, he was also fully human.

Second, in this event, John the Baptist gave his "seal of approval" to Jesus. John was a person with a great following, so when he told the listeners that Jesus was much greater than he was, that was saying a lot. Even in our own time we humans take great stock in the "seal of approval" given by certain people. For example, whenever Oprah Winfrey recommends a book on her television show, the sales of the book skyrocket. Her opinion made a big difference to millions of people. The same thing was true with the words of John the Baptist.

And third, in this event, we get a glimpse of God as a Trinity of Persons. God the Holy Spirit appears as a dove, God the Son gets baptized in the river, and God the Father speaks through the clouds informing the people that Jesus is indeed his Son.

Today, in Catholic and Orthodox Christianity, as well as in most but not all of Protestant Christianity, baptism is our initiation into the Christian Church. In our baptism we become part of the Body of Christ on Earth. We become special children of God.

Unfortunately, though, some of us forget just how special we are. One Christian man who never did forget was George Washington Carver.

George Washington Carver, who lived from 1864 to 1943, was an African-American man of humble origins who became famous for his scientific research in the field of agriculture. Through his research at Iowa State University and Tuskegee Institute in Alabama, George discovered hundreds of uses for peanuts as well as sweet potatoes and other crops. He also taught farmers how to rotate their crops so that the soil could be enriched rather than depleted.

One day, George received an invitation to come to Washington, D.C. to address the United States House of Representatives. When he arrived at the Capitol, he watched while other invited guests before him testified. He was amazed at how rudely the Congressmen treated these guests, all of them white. If the Congressmen treated the white men so badly, he could not imagine how terribly they would treat him as a black man.

Then, however, George Washington Carver remembered something very important. He remembered that he was baptized in Jesus Christ and was, therefore, a very special person. He was a special child of God and a member of the Body of Christ on Earth. He was a Christian.

When it was his turn to testify on his research, he was told that he had ten minutes to talk. Ten minutes to talk about his life's work was all he was granted. But George began talking about his research with peanuts and the three hundred uses he had discovered for them. He talked about his agricultural research. The Congressmen, not used to listening to a black man, were fascinated with what he was saying. Therefore, when his ten minutes were up, they gave him ten more minutes, and then ten more minutes, until he had been permitted to talk for over an hour and forty-five minutes.

With only a few exceptions, George Washington Carver refused to sell his ideas, for he believed that God gave them to him. As a child of God, he was not entitled to sell these gifts. George had a profound appreciation of his Christian vocation. On his grave is written, "He could have added fortune to fame, but caring for neither, he found happiness and honor in being helpful to the world."

Although it is unlikely that any of us here will ever be as famous as George Washington Carver, every one of us who is Christian has exactly the same calling or vocation that George had, that is, to be a disciple of Christ. And our vocation, like that of George's, comes from our baptism.

How we live our lives as Christians differs. We have different occupations, for example, but each of us is called to serve Jesus Christ. That is our basic vocation.

As we continue our life journeys this week, it would be a good idea to ask ourselves how we live our vocations as Christians. How do we try to make this a better world?

And that is the good news I have for you on this Feast of the Baptism of the Lord.

Part Two

LENT &
EASTER SEASONS

Chapter 9

1st Sunday of Lent - A
Temptation – People, Places & Things

Scripture:

- Genesis 2: 7-9; 3: 1-7
- Psalm 51: 3-4, 5-6a, 12-13, 14 & 17
- Romans 5: 12-19
- Matthew 4: 1-11

As we gather today to celebrate the Eucharist on this First Sunday of Lent, we hear the interesting story of Jesus being tempted by the devil in the desert. The devil tries to get Jesus to fall for three things: sensual appetites; power; and worldly riches. Jesus, being God, rejected all these temptations.

The concept of "temptation" is very important to Christians. In fact, it is so important that every single time we gather to celebrate Eucharist, we pray "...and lead us not into temptation" in the Lord's Prayer.

But what is temptation? In the usual context, temptation refers to enticements towards something evil.

Unfortunately, sin is often very attractive towards us. You may remember the old joke that says, "Everything I like is illegal, immoral, or fattening". The reason that the joke is funny is that it is so often true in our own lives.

Temptations, unfortunately, will always be with us. Although God guides our lives, he does not run our lives. That is our responsibility. When we realize that, and when we realize that it is our job to fight temptation, we come to realize that we need to recognize sources of temptation and design practical solutions to counteract them. Today, let's look at three common sources of temptation: people, places, and things.

First, people can be sources of temptation for us. Each year, for example, before Thanksgiving or Christmas advice columnists often hear from people who plan to visit relatives who bring out the very worst in them. They lament that some relatives "push their buttons" in such a way that they end up saying hurtful things to family members. Others find that there are people at work whom they detest so much they have a hard time being civil to them.

Other times, there are people who lead us into dangerous behavior. We find that whenever we are around them, we are tempted to engage in problematic behavior with them such as gossip or immoral behavior.

When we know what kind of people "bring out the devil in us," we can come up with strategies to lessen the chances of sin. Sometimes that means not being around such people.

Second, places can be problems for us. That is why Overeaters' Anonymous doesn't have meetings in bakeries and why Alcoholics' Anonymous doesn't have meetings in bars and taverns.

In current American society, dangerous "places" can also include web sites on our computers. For example, because of the ease with which we can order things online, many people engage in impulse spending that way. It is so easy to push a button. Others find that the Internet has many chat rooms or pornographic sites that lead them into dangerous territory. Some people find themselves making intimate friends on the Internet that lead to illicit affairs, divorce, and even suicide and homicide.

In discussing "places" as sources of temptation, I would also add the element of "time." For example, each of has what is known as a circadian cycle. That means that there are certain times of day when we are at our best and at our worst. I, for example, have tremendous energy at 5 a.m. but am basically a zombie in the afternoon hours. Because I know this, I schedule important work in the morning and avoid anything important in the afternoon if I can at all help it. Therefore, if I have to do something in the afternoon, especially if it something that I don't particularly like to do, I have to be extra careful to be on guard to be pleasant to those around me.

Another example of time problems would be going out of your house at night when you fully realize that it is during night hours that you have, in the past, gotten into trouble.

The third big source of temptation is "things." In current American society, many people have a very difficult time distinguishing between "wants" and "needs." There are very few genuine "needs" in our lives aside from air, water, shelter, some clothes, transportation, a job, and food.

As Americans, every imaginable thing under the sun surrounds us, and because most of us can charge things instead of having to pay cash for them, we are constantly tempted to buy beyond our means.

In the past, I used to watch two shows that dealt with financial problems that Americans get into because of incorrect spending: "The Suze Orman Show" and "Till Debt Do Us Part." Both shows demonstrated how otherwise intelligent people could be reckless with money. This recklessness can wreak havoc with mental health, spirituality, marriage, jobs, and other realms of life.

So people, places, and things can all be sources of temptation to us. When we realize which sources are most problematic for us, we can take measures to minimize their effects on us.

As we continue our life journeys this week, it would be a good idea to examine our lives and ask how we handle temptations. What are the biggest temptation sources in our lives? How do we handle them successfully and not so successfully?

And that is the good news I have for you on this First Sunday of Lent.

Chapter 10

2nd Sunday of Lent - A
Phelps and the Transfiguration

Scripture:

- Genesis 12: 1-4a
- Psalm 33: 4-5, 18-19, 20 & 22
- 2 Timothy 1: 8b-10
- Matthew 17: 1-9

As we gather to celebrate the Eucharist on this Second Sunday of Lent, we once again hear the interesting story of the Transfiguration of Jesus. In this story, Jesus goes on a mountain with Peter, James and John. Suddenly, Moses and Elijah appear with Jesus. Quickly, the apostles want to build three tents: one for Jesus, one for Elijah, and one for Moses. "Building a tent" refers to giving great honor to a person. But as the apostles were thinking of giving honor to the three men, a voice came from a cloud saying, "This is my beloved Son, with whom I am well pleased; listen to him." The disciples fell down in fear, but Jesus told them not to be afraid. When they arose, both Elijah and Moses had disappeared, and only Jesus remained.

Bible scholars who devote their whole lives to studying sacred scripture are baffled in some ways by this story. They don't know, for example, when it occurred. For you and me, though, that is not important. What is important is what message we can glean from the story.

The Transfiguration story has a very clear message. The Old Testament law, represented by Moses, is now gone, and the prophecy of the Old Testament, represented by Elijah, is also gone. Jesus is now all that we need. Jesus is God. Jesus is the fulfillment of the Old Testament law and prophecy.

Unfortunately, though, through the ages people and things other than Jesus have distracted Christians. As a result, their Christian faith became endangered. Sometimes, it even became so twisted that it became the very opposite of Jesus' message of love. That happened in our own times and in our own country to a man who built his entire life around hatred. The man's name was Fred Phelps.

Fred Phelps was born in Meridian, Mississippi to a homemaker and a railroad worker. When he was 16 years old, he was admitted to the prestigious West Point Military Academy. Fred, however, as a result of attending a Methodist revival meeting, felt that God wanted him to be a preacher instead of a soldier. After attending many schools for a few semesters each, Fred eventually became a lawyer as well as a preacher.

As a lawyer, initially he defended the civil rights of African Americans and women. He even won awards for his work. But in time, he turned from being a champion of civil rights to an enemy of civil rights. The beginning of Fred's journey into hate was seen as early as 1951 when he was a student at John Muir College. At that time, *Time* magazine ran a piece on Fred in which he condemned the faculty and students of the school for what he interpreted to be evil.

In 1955, he founded the Westboro Baptist Church in Wichita, Kansas. Though he claimed to be part of the Primitive Baptist movement, his church was not affiliated with any known organized denomination. Though Fred Phelps died in March of 2014, his church lives on. Today, this church, composed mostly of family members, has fewer than 100 members. Despite its tiny size, it is known throughout the land as a center of radical hate. Though its major focus is hatred of gay American men, it also condemns Catholic Christians and almost all Protestant denominations. It condemns the United States of America and its leaders. It condemns members of the military and those who support the military. Fred himself taught that evangelist Billy Graham was the greatest false prophet since Old Testament times. Fred taught that Jesus came only for some people, not all people.

His Westboro Baptist Church is most famous for picketing at funerals with hate signs. The theology of hate of this "church" is very close to that of Nazism of the Twentieth century.

When we encounter someone like Fred Phelps who preached hate instead of love—all in the name of Jesus Christ—we shudder. We recoil. We look on in disgust and anger and pity. And we sometimes think, "That could never happen to me."

But of course many people do turn away from Jesus. Because this happens in very small degrees, they often don't realize it is happening. So what kind of things can detract people from making Jesus the center point of their lives?

Some people fall in love with things of the world such as money, houses, or extravagant lifestyles. They put the material world ahead of Jesus.

Some fall in love with power or political parties.

Others fall in love with themselves and their pseudo-sanctity. Such people look down on other people whom they judge to be spiritually or morally inferior to them.

Some fall in love with rules and regulations, becoming rigorists who disdain such human qualities as sensitivity and compassion that Jesus taught.

There are even some who fall in love with religious leaders or churches, taking them as replacements for Jesus.

The good news, though, is that we do not have to replace Jesus as the center of our lives. However, because of all the temptations to replace Jesus with people and things around us, we need to be ever vigilant, always being the guardians of our souls.

And that is the good news I have for you on this Second Sunday of Lent.

Story source:

- Daniel Burke. "Westboro church founder Fred Phelps dies." CNN. March 25, 2014.

Chapter 11

3rd Sunday of Lent - A
Iraqis and the Well

Scripture:

- Exodus 17: 3-7
- Psalm 95: 1-2, 6-7c, 7d-9
- Romans 5: 1-2, 5-8
- John 4: 5-42

As we gather today to celebrate the Eucharist on this Third Sunday of Lent, we hear the famous story of Jesus greeting the Samaritan woman at the well. This was, of course, a very strange thing for Jesus to do, for Jews usually did not interact with Samaritans. But even stranger, Jesus told the woman that he was the Messiah and had water that would give eternal life. Furthermore, this water was for everyone, not just the Jews.

This was big news indeed. Not only did the Jews think they were the only ones that God loved, they never thought that the promised Messiah would be for other people also. Even today, many people think they are the "chosen people." That is what some Catholic Christians thought in the following story.

There was once a very progressive suburban parish that had lots of committees and ministries. The teenagers built homes for the poor in the mountains of Appalachia, the adults ran soup kitchens for the homeless, many of the parishioners participated in clothes drives and blood drives, and they were generous towards the poor. As a result of their good deeds, the people of the parish were very proud of themselves.

But one day, a new family moved into the parish, and the parishioners did not know what to make of them. They had dark skin and talked with a strange accent and had lots of money. They were not African-American, and they were not Hispanic. They quickly improved the landscape of their yard and fixed up their large new home to look very beautiful. They had three cars: a Lexus, a Cadillac, and a Lincoln. The people of the parish noted that the new family had three children, a mother and father, and two grandparents, and that lots of company visited the home.

The parishioners began to form unfounded guesses about this new family, and rumors started. Some said they were probably oil millionaires from Saudi Arabia. Others said they might be members of some foreign gangster family. But the one rumor that turned out to be true was that the family was Iraqi. Suddenly the neighbors became very suspicious. They called the FBI and reported the family. "They are probably spies," the neighbors said. "Their Lincoln looks like it might contain bombs" others said.

Soon, the neighbors set up a "neighborhood watch" to keep a close eye on these Iraqis just to make sure there were no suspicious meetings taking place. The neighbors drove by the house day and night to keep track of these suspected terrorists. After all, they reasoned, if they're Iraqi, they are bound to be up to no good.

Well, soon the summer turned into fall, and the parish school opened for another school year. And whom do you think showed up on the first day of school in crisp new Catholic school uniforms? You guessed it! The three Iraqi children!

A group of concerned parents got together in the parking lot of the parish and decided they had better inform the pastor about non-Christian kids entering the school. But when they reported this to the pastor, he informed them that the Iraqi children were not only Christian, but they were Catholic Christians. In fact, he told the parents, Catholic Christianity had been established long before missionaries brought Catholic Christianity to Ireland!

As it turned out, the family owned a chain of camera stores, and that is why they had so much money. The older girl turned out to be quite an excellent basketball player and was a great asset to the parish girls' basketball team. The family, in fact, turned out to be one of the most generous and active families the parish had ever seen!

This story, and the story of Jesus at the well, reminds Catholic Christians of many things. Here are just three of them.

First, Catholic Christians pray for the salvation of all people. "All" means every human being that ever lived, all who are living now, and every human being who will live in the future. In fact, we pray for the salvation of all humanity because we believe that with God, all things are possible, and we believe that God's love and mercy have no limits. This Catholic Christian perspective is diametrically different from Biblical literalism and fundamentalism.

Second, of all the people on Earth, Catholic Christians should always strive to be inclusive instead of exclusive. After all, "catholic" means "universal." We should always be ready to welcome the stranger, and we should always try to find Christ who lives in every person. Our parishes should be welcome ports for all of life's travelers. After all, that is the basic Christian commandment, to treat others as we wish to be treated. As Jesus said, whatever we do to others, we are actually doing it to him— whether good or evil.

And third, Catholic Christians are called to take Christ's message of love and welcome to the whole world. That means that we should work to encourage all societies of the world to treat every human being with dignity and respect.

As we continue our life journeys this week, it would be a good idea to take some time to examine our own lives. How do we practice the love ethic of Jesus towards others, especially those who may be different from us?

And that is the good news I have for you on this Third Sunday of Lent.

Story source: Andrew Greeley, "Iraqi Christians," in a homily for Lent 3 on the Internet.

Chapter 12

4th Sunday of Lent – A
Spiritual Blindness

Scripture:

- 1 Samuel 16: 1b, 6-7, 10-13a
- Psalm 23: 1-3a, 3b-4, 5, 6
- Ephesians 5: 8-14
- John 9: 1-41

Today as we gather to celebrate the Eucharist, we hear the wonderful story of a man who was born blind. Jesus cures him.

Now before we explore this passage and its meaning, there are some things we must remember. First, this passage was written by John, the most mystical of the gospel writers. In fact, when seminarians study to become priests, they have one course called the "Synoptic Gospels" which includes those of Matthew, Mark, and Luke, and a totally separate course in the Gospel of John. That is in part because John's writing is very complex.

John writes on at least three different levels, so we can never take John's stories literally. For example, when John speaks of "Jerusalem," sometimes he means the city by that name. Sometimes he means the center of Judaism. And at other times he means heaven. If we don't understand this, we can become very confused.

John also uses the symbols of light and darkness, night and day. So when John says someone came to a well at noon, it does not necessarily mean it was 12 p.m. It could mean that Jesus was present at the well, the One who is all light.

In today's Gospel, "blindness" could mean the man was either sightless at birth, or it could mean that he was spiritually blind. Spiritual blindness is something all of us have from time to time. We can't see our faults. We are in the dark about them.

Many people go through life thinking they have 20/20 spiritual eyesight. They believe they can easily see their faults and their virtues. Sometimes, though, they are mistaken.

In the following Hasidic story, a rabbi gives his followers some insight into the concept of spiritual blindness versus spiritual sight.

There was once a rabbi who asked his students this question: "How can we determine the hour of dawn, when the night ends and the day begins?"

One student answered, "When from a distance you can distinguish between a dog and a sheep."

The rabbi said, "No, that is not the answer."

Another student said, "Is it when one can distinguish between a fig tree and a grapevine?"

The rabbi once again answered, "No."

After many students attempted to answer the question without success, the students begged the rabbi to tell them the answer.

The wise rabbi said, "You can tell when the night ends and the day begins when you can look into the eyes of human beings and you have enough light inside of you to recognize them as your brothers or sisters. Until you can do that, it is night, and darkness is still with you."

Like St. John, the rabbi in this story uses the concept of "light" and "day" to refer to something spiritual, something good. Likewise, he uses the concept of "darkness" and "night" to refer to something negative.

As Catholic Christians, we are called to be "lights to the world." That means that we need to be able to distinguish light from darkness, and that we are willing to put the light inside us. It also means we recognize and dispel the darkness that lurks in our souls.

Fortunately for Catholic Christians, we have a special method of continually searching for light and dispelling darkness. This process is known as an "examination of conscience."

An examination of conscience is a process of taking stock of our spiritual journey. People look at their souls to determine what wrong they have done. Sometimes this process is called "identifying the weeds" of our "spiritual gardens."

The two types of "spiritual weeds" we can identify are acts of commission and acts of omission.

Acts of commission are actions we took which are evil. Some common examples would be gossiping to hurt another person, stealing money or other items, lying, physically harming another person, taking God's name in vain, copying someone else's homework, driving while drunk, and many other actions.

Acts of omission, on the other hand, are cases in which we were morally obligated to do something but failed to do so. We might see someone on the side of the road who needs help, but we ignore the person. Or we see people who are sad and could use cheering up but we fail to smile and put in a good word to them. We may encounter someone without something to eat and fail to share our food. In short, we failed to recognize others as our brothers or sisters.

Although it is always wise to do an examination of conscience before celebrating Reconciliation, it is also a good idea to do this every night before going to bed. This does not have to be a complex process. Simply ask yourself, "What did I do wrong today? What kinds of things should I have done but failed to do?" Then, after we have finished with our examination of conscience, we promise to do better tomorrow.

And that is the good news I have for you on this Fourth Sunday in Lent.

Story source: Old Hasidic tale, in Anthony Castle's *A Treasury of Quips, Quotes and Anecdotes for Preachers and Teachers*, 1998, p. 499.

Chapter 13

5th Sunday of Lent - A
The Resurrection Theme

Scripture:

- Ezekiel 37: 12-14
- Psalm 130: 1-2, 3-4, 5-6ab & 7a, 7b-8
- Romans 8: 8-11
- John 11: 1-45

As we come together to celebrate the Eucharist on this Fifth Sunday of Lent, we hear the Gospel story of Jesus raising his friend, Lazarus, from the dead. In the early Catholic Church, this miracle was a very popular subject for religious art.

When we read this story, two messages jump out at us right away. First, to do such a miracle, Jesus must have been God as well as man; in other words, the story shows Jesus' divinity. Second, Jesus loved his friend, Lazarus, very much.

But the obvious messages are only part of the story. For Catholic Christians, this story is about the resurrection experiences we can enjoy all through our life cycle. In this sense, resurrection is a symbol for the Christian belief that goodness will overcome evil, light will overcome darkness, and life will overcome death. In other words, the Catholic vision is truly a romantic vision, a "happily ever after" view of reality.

In the following story, we get a glimpse in the "happy ending" that is always present in a truly Catholic story.

Long ago and far away, there was a king who decided to conduct an experiment. He placed a huge boulder in the middle of a roadway, then hid and watched to see if anyone would remove the boulder.

Many people of the kingdom came by and simply walked around the boulder. Many of them were angry about the boulder being in the road, and they loudly blamed the king for not keeping the road free from obstacles. None of them, however, did anything to clear the road of the boulder.

Then a poor peasant farmer came down the road carrying a load of vegetables on his back. When he came to the boulder, he removed his burden and began trying to remove the big stone to the side of the road. After a lot of pushing and straining, he finally succeeded.

As he picked up his load of vegetables to continue his journey, he noticed a purse lying in the road where the boulder had been. The purse contained gold coins worth a fortune. It also contained a note from the king saying that the gold was for the person who removed the boulder from the road. The poor peasant farmer was no longer poor, and he lived happily ever after.

The peasant farmer learned what many others have learned through the ages: every obstacle presents an opportunity to improve one's condition.

From this story and the story of Jesus raising his friend Lazarus from the dead, we can learn many things about the theme of resurrection.

First, Catholic Christians, like nearly all other types of Christians, believe that we experience death and resurrection in the Sacrament of Baptism. At Baptism, we "die with Christ" so that we can "rise with Christ." At our baptism, we are born again into a new life, the life of the Spirit. At baptism, original sin is removed. And if the person being baptized has committed other sins, all of these are automatically removed. Further, the Sacrament of Baptism is the key to all other sacraments, for it is only through this sacrament that the other ones are possible.

Second, as Catholic Christians, we believe that we have unlimited chances to experience resurrection in our lives. Every day, for example, we get a new chance to live our lives in a different way. Every day we can choose to be better persons than we were the day before. That is why the Church encourages Catholic Christians to live an "examined life," a life based on continual spiritual growth. For example, it is always a good idea to conduct an "examination of conscience" every night before we go to bed. In this examination of conscience, we look back over the day to see what we did well, what we did wrong, and what good things we failed to do. After identifying such things, we make a promise to God to do better tomorrow. In this way, we are always trying to rid spiritual weeds from the gardens of our souls. And we know that it is much easier to get rid of weeds when they begin to sprout up than after they have taken root and multiplied.

For Catholic Christians, the rising from sin to grace is so important that Jesus gave us the Sacrament of Reconciliation for us to enjoy. It is a precious sacrament in which we can experience the death of the old and the rebirth of the good any time we want it. And it is free!

Finally, for Catholic Christians, the death of the body is not the end of the story. Rather, the death of the body signals the birthday of our eternal life in the hereafter. Furthermore, Catholic Christians also believe that at the end of time, even the body—in a glorified state—will also rise. And unlike many peoples of the world, including many non-Catholic Christians, Catholic Christians ask God to save all people, not just a select group. After all, God's love and mercy have no limits, and with God all things are possible.

What role does the resurrection theme play in your daily life and vision of reality?

And that is the good news I have for you on this Fifth Sunday of Lent.

Story source: Anonymous, "Obstacle or opportunity?" in Brian Cavanaugh's *Fresh Packet of Sower's Seeds: Third Planting,* 1994, #51, p. 45.

Chapter 14

Palm Sunday - A
Being Prepared for Change

Scripture:

- Isaiah 50: 4-7
- Psalm 22: 8-9, 17-18a, 19-20, 23-24
- Philippians 2: 6-11
- Matthew 26: 14-27: 66

Today we celebrate Palm Sunday of the Passion of the Lord. This day marks the beginning of Holy Week, the most sacred week of the Church Year.

At the beginning of this Mass, we heard of the triumphant entry of Jesus into Jerusalem. There he was hailed as a king, and the people were singing and honoring him as the Son of David.

But later, the people turned on him, torturing and then killing him. Fortunately, though, we know the end of the story: Jesus rose from the dead.

What we can learn from the readings today is that we must always be prepared for change in our lives. If we are having particularly good times, we need to know that they will not always last, that sorrow will visit our doorstep. Likewise, when we are in times of turmoil, we need to remember that peace will return. In other words, change is inevitable in this life. The only constant is that a loving God is watching over us every minute of every day, whether we are walking on the sunny side of the street or are caught up in the storms of life.

That is the good news I have for you on this Palm Sunday of the Lord's Passion.

Chapter 15

Easter – A
A Soldier Comes Home

Scripture:

- Acts of the Apostles 10: 34a, 37-43
- Psalm 118: 1-2, 16-17, 22-23
- 1 Corinthians 5: 6b-8
- John 20: 1-9

Today we celebrate the Feast of the Resurrection of Jesus from the dead, Easter. And on behalf of all of us in our parish, I wish you and those you love a very Happy and Holy Easter Day and Easter Season. I pray that God will shower you with special blessings during this holy time.

Easter, as you know, is the greatest Feast of the Church Year. In fact, in the early days of the Church, the Church Fathers decided that they would replace the Sabbath (Saturday) with Sunday (The Lord's Day) as the day they would devote to honoring God. This custom has continued to this very day. And for Catholic Christians, like their Hebrew ancestors, feast days begin at sundown the day before.

Today is the day we celebrate Jesus rising from the dead. But Easter is more than just that historical event. It is more than a one-time thing that forms a basic part of our Christian faith. Rather, the good news of the Resurrection is the template that we can use in our daily lives, for we can always be transformed or resurrected. That is what the people discovered in the following story by Fr. Andrew Greeley.

There was once a young man whom I'll call Edward who left his family and friends to join the army. Unfortunately he was captured by the enemy and spent a few years as a prisoner of war. His family and friends, however, were told by the army that Edward had been killed in action.

Everyone who loved Edward mourned for him. But then, little by little, they began to move on with their lives. His girl friend, for example, became engaged to another man, and his parents gave away all his clothing. Though everyone had loved Edward, they basically wrote him out of their lives, even if not from their memories.

Then one day, to the astonishment of everyone, Edward returned home. He didn't seem at all like the teenager who had gone off to war. He was thinner and looking a bit haggard, but he was now much more mature and self-confident and very happy. As a child, he was not someone who joked or smiled much, but now he was witty and outgoing. The quiet teenage soldier who had left a few years earlier, now returned as a mature man who radiated joy.

His friends were amazed at this remarkable change. The old Edward was truly gone, and a new one had appeared. The new Edward, for example, congratulated his girl friend on her upcoming wedding and shook hands cordially with her fiancé. And this he did with great sincerity.

All of Edward's friends thought something was wrong with him, so they went to see the parish priest. The priest simply smiled and said, "The old Edward is dead, and the new Edward is born. And isn't that a terrific reflection of the Resurrection that is the center of our faith!"

This wonderful resurrection story, coupled with Jesus' rising from the dead, teaches us many things. Here are just three.

First, good things can come from bad times. That is the theme of the Resurrection. And that truly is good news, because for Catholic Christians, bad times are never to be the end of the story. As Catholic Christians, our view of reality is always a "happily ever after" one.

In daily life, we see this principal operating all around us. People in Alcoholics Anonymous, for example, often talk about being a "grateful recovering alcoholic." What they are "grateful" for is not alcoholism, or even that they surmounted it, but the fact that because of the disease, they were led to a type of spirituality called the 12-Step way of life. And from living this type of practical spirituality, they found God and a joyful way of living. Without the disease, they might never have discovered this joy or grown spiritually.

Second, we have many opportunities to experience resurrection or transformation in our lives. Perhaps we want to lose weight or get more exercise or cut down on stress or become less of a procrastinator. We can transform our lives by taking concrete steps to change the way we are living and thus meet our specific goals.

And third, it is never too late to experience resurrection, to transform our lives from bad to good. Every day is a like a pure blank page that God gives us in our book of life. No matter what the past pages of our lives look like, today's page can be whatever we want it to be. Transforming our lives is always an option that we have every single day. What an amazing concept that is! Every day we get to be different, to be better, to turn lemons into lemonade! Every day we get to be "lights to the world" in new and exciting ways. The only limits we have are the limits of our imaginations.

This week as we begin the long Easter Season, it would be a good idea to take some quiet time to reflect on our own lives. What kinds of bad things have we experienced that led to good things? What kinds of ways would we like to transform our lives? And what's stopping us?!

And that is the good news I have for you on this Easter Sunday.

Story source: "A Soldier Comes Home," from Andrew M. Greeley's Easter homily of 2000 on the Internet.

Chapter 16

2nd Sunday of Easter – A
The Magic Castle

Scripture:

- Acts of the Apostles 2: 42-47
- Psalm 118: 2-4, 13-15, 22-24
- 1 Peter 1: 3-9
- John 20: 19-31

As we gather together to celebrate the Eucharist on this Second Sunday of Easter, also called Divine Mercy Sunday, we read in the Gospel of John how Jesus instituted what today we call the Sacrament of Reconciliation. After breathing on his disciples, Jesus said, "Receive the Holy Spirit. Whose sins you forgive are forgiven them, and whose sins you retain are retained" (John 20: 22-23).

For two thousand years, now, Catholic Christians have treasured this gift and celebrated it in various ways. Some people, however, fail to treasure this incredible gift. That is what we see in the following story by Vernon Howard.

There was once a weary traveler who was wandering down a dark and scary road in a forest. He didn't know where he was or where he was going. The only thing he knew for sure was that he was very lost and very scared and very hungry.

Suddenly, as he rounded a bend in the forest path, he saw an incredible castle. The castle was brightly lit, and over the entrance was a "Welcome" sign. When he knocked on the door, a castle resident gave him a warm welcome and told him to come in and make himself at home. The traveler knew that he had reached a place of rest and peace, and he was no longer afraid. In fact, his heart was filled with joy.

But one thing seemed very strange to him. As he looked out a window of the castle, he saw many lost travelers who were walking right by the castle as if they didn't even see it. When the traveler asked the castle resident about this strange behavior, the resident explained the whole mystery to him.

"You see," began the castle resident, "this is no ordinary castle. This is a magic castle. Only those who realize they are lost and admit that they have lost their way can even see this castle. People who pretend to know where they are going or who demand everything their own way cannot see the castle. Because you were honest in admitting that you were lost, the castle was visible to you. Therefore, my friend, welcome to this castle, for all the riches of this magic castle are yours for the taking!"

The magic castle may be likened to the Sacrament of Reconciliation. This has also been called the Sacrament of Penance or Confession. But because reconciliation is the truly joyful part of the sacrament,

"Reconciliation" is the name preferred today. The "riches" of this magic castle are the graces that come from the mercy and forgiveness of God.

In the early days of the Church, when people wanted to celebrate this sacrament, they told their sins in front of the whole Christian community. Today, that would be quite impossible because one out of every six or seven human beings on the planet is a Catholic Christian, and more than one billion people could not get together to listen to one another's sins!

Today Catholic Christians usually celebrate the sacrament in a one-to-one setting with the priest or in a communal reconciliation service (such as during Advent or Lent) of which a one-to-one interaction with a priest is part.

Recently, in our parish, children who are celebrating First Communion also celebrated the Sacrament of Reconciliation. And as I told them, all sacraments are supposed to be joyful. There is no such thing as a "scary" sacrament.

To celebrate this sacrament, Catholic Christians are asked to do four things. First, we examine our consciences to see what we sins we may have. We may discover sins of commission, such as gossiping, or sins of omission, such as failing to be generous. Second, we have sorrow for our sins. When I was a little boy, I thought this sorrow was an emotional thing, and I certainly didn't feel that kind of sorrow. Sister Annella, my second grade teacher, assured me that one didn't have to cry to be sorry. Sorrow is a cognitive thing, not an emotional thing. Third, we confess our sins to an ordained priest or bishop. This person represents both the Church and Christ. As the Catechism of the Catholic Church says, "Only God can forgive sins." The priest is the instrument that God uses to assure people that God loves them and forgives them. And fourth, we do some kind of "penance" such as saying one Our Father.

But is the Sacrament of Reconciliation the only way that God forgives our sins? No. We are forgiven in many ways. As we read in Sacred Scripture, we can achieve forgiveness through all good works, through prayer, through fasting, and through being charitable to our neighbor. The Church teaches us that every sacramental act, especially the Eucharist, can forgive sin.

If this is so, what is so great about the Sacrament of Reconciliation? One of the best ways of understanding this is summed up in a story that a monsignor friend of mine tells. There was once a young student in a Catholic school who desperately wanted to celebrate Reconciliation with his Catholic classmates. There were just two problems. First, he was not a Catholic. And second, his father was a Baptist minister. The teacher was very curious why this little boy wanted to celebrate this sacrament. He said, "Well, when I say 'I'm sorry' to God, I *think* he forgives me, but I'm never sure. But when Catholic kids go to Confession, they *know* that God has forgiven them."

As we continue our life journeys this week, it would be a good idea to take some time to reflect on the Sacrament of Reconciliation. What riches are just waiting for us if we just enter into this magic castle?

And that is the good news I have for you on this Second Sunday of Easter.

Story source: Vernon Howard, "The Magic Castle," in Brian Cavanaugh's *The Sower's Seeds,* 1990, 29, pp. 26-27.

Chapter 17

3rd Sunday of Easter - A
Emmaus and the Bible

Scripture:

- Acts of the Apostles 2: 14, 22-33
- Psalm 16: 1-2a & 5, 7-8, 9-10, 11
- 1 Peter 1: 17-21
- Luke 24: 13-35

As we gather to celebrate the Eucharist today, we hear the famous Gospel passage that has come to be called "The Emmaus Story." In this story, two disciples were walking along from Jerusalem to Emmaus, a town seven miles from Jerusalem. They were talking about Jesus' crucifixion and the fact that his body was now missing.

As they walked along, suddenly another man joined them and asked them what they were talking about. They were amazed that he didn't know, so they told him about how they were followers of Jesus and had hoped that he was the Messiah and how he had been killed and how now his body was missing. And Jesus, whom they did not recognize, began to explain the Bible to them.

When they got to their house, they invited Jesus to dine with them. At the table, Jesus took bread, blessed it, broke it, and gave it to them. With that, they recognized him. Just as suddenly as he had appeared, he vanished. Then they knew for sure that Jesus had indeed risen from the dead.

This passage contains many elements to preach about. Today I'll talk about what Jesus was doing as he walked along with the disciples, unpacking the treasures of the Bible. These treasures are ours for the taking, but sometimes we don't appreciate this. That is what happened to the man in the following story.

There was once a man who was walking by himself in a desert, when suddenly he heard a voice from the sky say, "Pick up some pebbles, put them in your pocket, and tomorrow you will be both sorry and glad."

The man did as the mysterious voice said. He stooped down, picked up some pebbles, and put them in his pocket.

The next morning, when the man woke up, he reached into his pocket. He was amazed to find that during the night while he was sleeping, the pebbles had turned into diamonds and emeralds and rubies. He was, just as the voice had predicted, both sad and glad. He was obviously glad that the pebbles turned out to be precious gems, but he was sad that he had not picked up more.

And so it is with Sacred Scripture. The Bible, which is a collection of sacred books, is a treasure trove of precious gems. And the precious gems it contains are ours for the taking. There is plenty for each and every one of us, and they are available to us every single day.

The Bible intimidates many Catholic Christians. They feel they don't know enough, that the contents are over their heads. This is indeed a strange idea considering it was the early Catholic Christians who wrote the New Testament books of the Bible!

Though there are many obstacles in the minds of people who don't read the Bible, one very common obstacle is how to approach the content of the Bible. How should one read it? This is not as difficult a question as it may first appear.

There are two main ways to read the Bible, and both of them are correct. They each have a different purpose. We may approach the Bible as a window or as a mirror.

When we approach the Bible as a window, we are asking ourselves this question: What did the original authors mean by what they wrote? When we use this approach, we need to rely on people called exegetes, or Bible scholars, who devote their whole lives to studying the Scriptures. They tell us things that the average person does not know. They can talk about the social and cultural meanings various words had in the time and place they were written. For example, for an American in the twenty-first century, an "eye of a needle" refers to something grandma uses to sew up socks with holes in them. But the "eye of a needle" in Biblical times referred to the low entrance of a gated city. Because they were low, camels had a hard time ducking down far enough to get though the needle. Without the insights of exegetes, we would probably not know this.

Besides exegetes, Catholic Christians also rely on the teaching authority of the Church itself to learn what various things mean in the Scripture.

People who are intent on approaching the Bible as a window engage in an academic exercise called Bible studies.

The second way of reading the Bible is to approach the Bible as a mirror. The purpose of this method is to ask ourselves how the Bible touches our hearts, our lives. Thus every person is an expert, for only an individual knows how a particular Bible passage touches his or her heart. I, for example, find great joy in hearing the story of the lost sheep and the good shepherd. I love hearing Jesus talk about forgiveness and mercy. I do not, however, have the slightest interest in hearing about the Battle of Amalek or the dimensions of Noah's ark.

As we continue our life journeys this week, it would be a good idea to ask ourselves how we can develop a greater love for the Bible and all the gems it contains.

And that is the good news I have for you on this Third Sunday of Easter.

Story source: Anonymous, "A Handful of Pebbles," in Brian Cavanaugh's *Sower's Seeds of Encouragement: Fifth Planting,* 1998, #38, pp. 33-34.

Chapter 18

4th Sunday of Easter – A
The Shepherd and the Wolf

Scripture:

- Acts of the Apostles 2: 14a, 36-41
- Psalm 23: 1-3a, 3b-4, 5, 6
- 1 Peter 2: 20b-25
- John 10: 1-10

As we come together today to celebrate the Eucharist on this Fourth Sunday of Easter, we hear Jesus talking about shepherds and sheep. As a result, this Sunday is also called Good Shepherd Sunday. The Catholic Church has named this World Day of Prayer for Vocations. And although all Christians have vocations or callings, the Church asks us to pray especially for those called to be shepherds: priests and bishops.

In the Catholic Church, ordained priests who head up parishes are called pastors, another word for shepherds. In this role, they are called to exercise the ministry of the word, the ministry of sacraments, and the ministry of community leadership. As shepherds, they are not only called upon to love and care for their flock, the sheep, but they are called to always be on the lookout for dangers that could harm the flock. To prepare men for ordination, the Church requires a very rigorous course of study that takes, at a bare minimum, eight years of full-time academic study after graduation from high school. Most men study much longer than that before ordination.

Although we could talk about any of the various roles the pastor has, today I want to talk about the role of protecting the flock from harm. Specifically, I wish to talk about the harm that can come from within the community in people that might be called "wolves in sheep's clothing." This image comes from the following tale from the Greek storyteller, Aesop.

There was once a wolf that very much wanted to get some sheep to eat. Unfortunately for the wolf, though, a very vigilant shepherd and his dogs protected the sheep. One day, however, the wolf found the skin of a sheep that had been flayed and discarded. So, the wolf put the sheep's skin over itself and walked among the sheep.

The little lamb that belonged to the sheep whose skin the wolf was wearing soon began to follow the wolf wherever it went. Soon the wolf led the little lamb away from the other sheep. When the little lamb and wolf were out of sight of the other sheep, the wolf had a delicious meal of lamb chops. The wolf continued deceiving other sheep and lambs, leading them away from the herd and then eating them.

The moral of the story is, of course, that appearances are deceiving.

Now in parish life, there are all kinds of dangers that can endanger a flock. Financial problems, internal dissent, inter-parish rivalry, poor pastoral leadership, and runaway gossip are just some examples of dangers that can threaten a parish. One of the worst kinds of dangers, though, is that of what I call the "wolf-in-sheep's-clothing" syndrome.

In this scenario, there is a person who comes into the parish community, often with great fanfare. Such people try to get into leadership positions in established ministries and, little by little, try to get the members of the ministry to follow them outside the parish structure. If members of the ministry refuse to follow them, they may leave the established ministry and try to establish one outside the parish structure.

These "wolves in sheep's clothing" usually have certain characteristics. Very commonly they are people who believe they have special powers or insights that others do not have. They often preach that God has chosen them to lead others as spiritual gurus. Usually these people do not have academic qualifications to make such claims, and they may give themselves titles such as "Brother," "Sister," or "Mother" even though they are not members of religious orders. They feel that they do not need to have academic preparation to be a leader, or to endure the discipline of a religious order because the Holy Spirit has directly infused them with special gifts that others do not have.

They often see themselves as holier than other people, and they frequently become very angry when they are challenged. As they "pick off" members of the parish community to follow them, they begin establishing little groups that meet in houses or garages. They usually operate in secret and are known for badmouthing pastors or other parish leaders.

Frequently they engage in practices that the Catholic Church would not approve their doing, things such as "exorcising demons" from people they believe are on the wrong spiritual path.

What confuses members of the flock the most is that such leaders often say very orthodox things such as: "join the parish," "go to Communion," "have your marriage blessed by the Church," and other good things. Because such leaders say good things, their followers often begin developing such a strong trust in them that they fail to recognize harmful things the leader says.

People who have encountered such "wolves in sheep's clothing" frequently report that in time, they begin to feel badly. They often are sick to their stomach or have headaches. They feel a lack of joy in their lives, and they realize their spiritual life is suffering. Eventually, they realize they have been duped and that the person who they thought was a genuine spiritual leader was actually a charlatan.

If you wonder about the person who is encouraging you to join groups outside the parish structure have the endorsement of the Catholic Church via the parish, please come and see me.

Though these "wolves in sheep's clothing" have been able to sow seeds of confusion and division through the centuries, the good news is that the shepherds have always been able to shine the light on them and end their twisted work.

On this World Day of Prayer for Vocations, let us pray that we will always have good shepherds for our parishes to protect the flock from all harm.

And that is the good news I have for you on this Fourth Sunday of Easter, Good Shepherd Sunday.

Chapter 19

5th Sunday of Easter – A
Called to Be a Disciple

Scripture:

- Acts of the Apostles 6: 1-7
- Psalm 33: 1-2, 4-5, 18-19
- 1 Peter 2: 4-9
- John 14: 1-12

As we gather to celebrate the Eucharist on this Fifth Sunday of Easter, we hear Peter telling us that we are a "chosen race, a royal priesthood, a holy nation, a people of his own...." (1 Peter 2: 9). In other words, we are called to live special lives, and that is something about which we need to be reminded every now and then. That is what the writer of the following story had in mind.

Once there was a very important writer who said that a great book requires a great theme. Unfortunately, many books do not have great themes, so they are not great literature. They will not be remembered through the ages.

The writer went on to say that people are like books. They, too, need great themes to be great people. A theme, in this instance, is a profound thread that weaves itself in one's life no matter what. It is the overriding concern, the principle that gives one's life a sense of purpose and meaning.

Many people have no theme. They simply drift through life attracted to trivial things, materialism, or selfishness. They have nothing outside of themselves that they feel passionate about.

Great people, however, have a strong sense of purpose and meaning in their lives. Sociologists and psychologists, like spiritual writers, talk about such people as being "self-actualized." Such people all have one thing in common: they are very passionate about something in life that is greater than they are. The great Indian leader, Gandhi, for example, lived a life driven by a desire for peace on Earth. Mother Teresa of Calcutta had a passion to serve the poorest of the poor, seeing Jesus in every face she encountered. Rev. Martin Luther King, Jr. lived a life driven by the desire to achieve equality under the law for all Americans, not just white ones.

But, you may say, those were extraordinary people. Could someone like me be called to greatness?

The answer is a resounding, "Yes!" True, none of us will probably ever achieve the fame of a Gandhi or a Mother Teresa or a Martin Luther King. That is not the point. The point is that we are called to live lives filled with a great theme, that is, lives filled with purpose and meaning. And how did I come to that conclusion?

That conclusion comes from today's three Scripture readings. In the Acts of the Apostles, for example, we hear the early members of our Church referred to as "disciples." A "disciple" is a student of a master, a person who studies the life and sayings of a master and tries to imitate the life and teaching of the master. For Christians, Jesus is the master we follow.

In the first letter of Peter, we hear that we are a "chosen race, a royal priesthood, a holy nation, a people of his own...." We are called to be no ordinary people; rather, we are called to live extraordinary lives by virtue of our royalty.

And finally, Jesus tells us that if we believe in him, we will be his disciples. He says, "Amen, amen, I say to you, whoever believes in me will do the works that I do, and will do greater ones than these because I am going to the Father" (John 14: 12).

In other words, we are called to be disciples. And who is called to be a disciple of Jesus? Every person who is baptized is a disciple of Jesus. At my previous parish, something very profound happened to me. I was saying good-bye to people as they left the church after one of the Masses, and I had on my vestments. A young boy came up to me, and with great respect in his eyes, asked me in a very reverential way, "Are you a disciple of Jesus?" This question pierced me to the heart. I answered, "Yes, I am. And guess what? You are too!" With that, his eyes became as big as saucers and a big smile broke out on his face. I went on to tell him, "Everyone who is baptized is a disciple of Jesus."

Later that evening, I began to reflect on my encounter with this boy. I began to think that if this boy doesn't know that he is a disciple, then probably other people don't know that either. Therefore, I better begin to preach more on what it is to be a disciple.

To be a disciple means to be a follower and student of Jesus. It means that no matter what happens in our lives, we have a sense of purpose and meaning. It means we model Jesus in everyday life. It means that we try to see Jesus in every person we meet. It means we forgive those who hurt us. It means we say we're sorry when we're wrong. It means we give thanks to God for all our blessings. It means we give freely of what we have to others, especially to those who have little. It means we take the talents that God gave us and develop them even further. It means that we advocate peace instead of conflict. It means that we are industrious in our lives and not lazy. It means we help others on their life's journey. It means that we follow Jesus and not become blinded by rules or regulations or earthly religious leaders. It means that we not judge others lest we be judged. It means accepting all humanity as our brothers and sisters.

This week, perhaps it would be good to take some time out to reflect on how we live our lives. How do we show we are disciples of Jesus? Do we have a great theme or passion in our lives? Or are we content to glide through life concerned only about our own happiness?

That is the good news I have for you on this Fifth Sunday of Easter.

Story source: Harry Huxhold, "To Have a Great Theme (adapted)," in Brian Cavanaugh's *Sower's Seeds that Nurture Family Values, Sixth Planting*, 2000, #3, p. 9.

Chapter 20

6th Sunday of Easter – A
St. Telemachus

Scripture:

- Acts of the Apostles 8: 5-8, 14-17
- Psalm 66: 1-3a, 4-5, 6-7a, 16 & 20
- 1 Peter 3: 15-18
- John 14: 15-21

As we gather to celebrate the Eucharist on this Sixth Sunday of Easter, we hear Peter telling us that as disciples, we should be ready to explain our faith to others, but that we are to do so gently. Peter says, "Always be ready to give an explanation to anyone who asks you for a reason for your hope, but do it with gentleness and reverence, keeping your conscious clear, so that, when you are maligned, those who defame your good conduct in Christ may themselves be put to shame" (1 Peter 3: 15-16).

For most of us, professing our Catholic Christian faith is usually not very dramatic. But for some people, like the man in the following story by Lee Christie, putting faith into action can actually cost a human life.

In the fourth century, there was a monk by the name of Telemachus. One day, Telemachus felt that God was calling him to go to Rome. Always ready to follow God's call, Telemachus put a few of his belongings into a traveling bag, threw it over his shoulder, and walked the dusty roads to Rome.

When he got to Rome, there was great excitement in the air and people were rushing to the amphitheater to see gladiators fight each other and wild animals. The people saw this as "entertainment" in those days.

Telemachus figured that that is why God had called him to go to Rome on that day, so he went to the amphitheater with about thousands of other people. The people cheered as the gladiators came out and shouted, "Hail Caesar! We die to the glory of Caesar!"

The little monk sat in silence and thought to himself how this violence against men was morally wrong. It was wrong for men to harm other men, and it was wrong to see killing as entertainment. Telemachus knew this was anti-Christian.

Suddenly, filled with the Holy Spirit, Telemachus got out of his seat, ran down the steps, climbed over the wall, and walked into the center of the amphitheater and stood in between two large gladiators who were about to harm each other. Putting his hands up, he meekly cried out, "In the name of Jesus Christ, stop!" The crowd laughed and jeered at Telemachus. One of the gladiators knocked Telemachus down, but Telemachus got up again and repeated, "In the name of Christ, stop." This time, the crowd began to chant for the gladiators to kill Telemachus. And that is exactly what a gladiator did when he ran his sword through

Telemachus' stomach. As the life ran out of him, St. Telemachus cried out one more time, "In the name of Christ, stop." With that, he died.

The crowd grew silent, and within minutes they began leaving the amphitheater. Thanks to St. Telemachus, this was the last gladiatorial contest in the history of the Roman Empire.

Although it is highly unlikely that God will call you and me to do something so heroic to show our faith, we too are called to profess our faith before others. Here are just three ways that we can profess our Catholic Christian faith in everyday life.

First, the best way is by becoming a living, walking homily. This means that we live our lives in such a way that people cannot help but be impressed. This is what Jesus called being a "light to the world."

We let our "light shine" in many ways. For example, we have a home filled with love and joy. We welcome everyone who comes to our home as though they were Jesus Christ because, in reality, Christ does live in each of us. We are hard workers in our jobs whether the boss is there or not. We are always willing to help our neighbors in need, whether the neighbors are those who live close to us or those in other countries.

In our leisure life, we should not be afraid to show our Catholic Christian faith. We should never be ashamed to make the Sign of the Cross in a restaurant before and after we pray. That is what *Catholic* Christians do.

Second, we should be able and willing to explain our Catholic Christian faith to others when they ask. If you don't know something about the faith that the people ask, don't make up an answer. Simply say, "I'm not really sure about the answer to your question, but I'll be happy to find out for you." Then, make sure you learn the answer from a reputable source such as the parish priest.

When we are called upon to share our faith, we should follow St. Peter's advice and share it with "gentleness and reverence." We should not get into hostile arguments with others. If others do get hostile and make fun of your faith, one way I have found effective in calming them down is to say, "Well, I don't know all about your faith tradition, but I can say this: If it produced such a fine person as yourself, it must have many good things about it."

And third, we profess our faith by registering in, and becoming involved in, a parish. The parish is where *Catholic* Christians live out their faith in community. That is where Catholic Christians grow and flourish. That is where we learn more about our faith. That is where we get new ideas to take home to our "domestic church," the family. That is where we celebrate the milestones of our lives and the lives of our loved ones. And remember, if you are not registered in the parish, you are not a member of the parish.

As we continue our life journeys this week, it would be a good idea to ask ourselves how we profess our Catholic Christian faith to the world around us.

And that is the good news I have for you on this Sixth Sunday of Easter.

Story source: Lee Christie, "Telemachus Goes to Rome," in Wayne Rice's *Hot Illustrations for Youth Talks,* Grand Rapids, Michigan: Zondervan Youth Specialties, 1993, pp. 195-197.

Chapter 21

Ascension - A
St. Francis Xavier

Scripture:

- Acts of the Apostles 1: 1-11
- Psalm 47: 2-3, 6-7, 8-9
- Ephesians 1: 17-23
- Matthew 28: 16-20

Today we celebrate the Feast of the Ascension. This is the day we remember Jesus' ascension into heaven after his appearances to the disciples following his crucifixion and resurrection. Now he is leaving them again. But before he ascends into heaven, he tells them to "Go, therefore, and make disciples of all nations, baptizing them in the name of the Father, and of the Son, and of the Holy Spirit, teaching them to observe all that I have commanded you. And behold, I am with you always, until the end of the age" (Matthew 28: 19-20).

For 2,000 years now, Catholic Christians have tried to follow this missionary commandment of Jesus. Most of us live out our faith quietly in our daily lives. Instead of taking our faith out into foreign lands, we express it in our parish communities and in our homes. We pass the faith along to our children and those who come to us. When asked about our faith in the workplace or in our leisure lives, we share it with others.

There have always been some Catholic Christians, however, who follow the missionary commandment of Jesus Christ in bolder and more literal ways. One of the most famous and successful examples of such a missionary was Francis Xavier.

Francis was born in 1506 in Spain to a wealthy family. When he was seventeen, he was sent to the University of Paris to study. There he met another young man who was also a Spanish nobleman, by the name of Ignatius of Loyola.

Ignatius had to work hard to persuade his friend Francis to give his life to Christ. But with persistence, Ignatius was successful. And in 1534 Ignatius and Francis, along with five other young men, vowed to serve Christ in a special way. They called their group the Society of Jesus, spiritual soldiers for Jesus Christ. All of the men were ordained as priests in Venice.

When he was thirty-five years old, Francis set sail for the East Indies as a Jesuit missionary. Though the king wanted to give him a servant and money, Francis refused the gifts. He said, "...the best means to acquire true dignity is to wash one's own clothes and boil one's own pot, unbeholden to anyone."

Despite severe seasickness, Francis preached every Sunday and cared for the slaves, convicts and others who were aboard the ship. The trip to the Indies took thirteen months because the ship had to winter in Africa.

After reaching his destination of Goa, India, Francis began living the life of a missionary. He ate only rice with water, slept on a mat on the floor, and baptized many people. Sometimes he baptized so many people in a day that he could hardly lift his arms from fatigue.

Unfortunately for Francis, he was not gifted at learning languages. He discovered, as many do, that it is much more difficult to learn a new language as an adult than it is as a child. Nevertheless, he continually struggled to learn enough to share the stories of Jesus, of God, of heaven to the people. And he was successful.

Much of Francis Xavier's missionary success was due not only to his love for the people, but also because he incorporated the cultural practices of the people into his missionary work. For example, in India he found that the religious poverty of the missionaries had a great appeal. In India, therefore, there was no problem, for he was always poor. But when he got to Japan, he discovered that holy poverty was held in contempt. Therefore, Francis used a different approach in Japan. He and his companions dressed up in their very best clothes and went to the ruler of the people. To the ruler he presented himself as a representative of the King of Portugal, and gave the ruler letters from authorities in India. He also gave the ruler some presents: a music box, a clock, and some glasses. With this approach, Francis Xavier won his way into the hearts of the Japanese rulers who, in turn, permitted his work to flourish.

Francis Xavier, the missionary who went to many lands for Christ, had one great desire: to go to China. However, when he was forty-six years old, he died on an island right off the coast of China. Only four people came to his burial.

Francis Xavier was declared a saint of the Catholic Church in 1622 along with St. Ignatius of Loyola, St. Teresa of Avila, and St. Philip Neri. His feast day is December 3. He is a Patron Saint of foreign missionaries and Japan.

The life of St. Francis Xavier shows us many things. Here are just three.

First, we see the power of prayer and persistence. It was through his friend's continual persistence that Francis Xavier finally turned his heart to Christ. We, too, should never give up on changing hearts through our prayers.

Second, St. Francis Xavier followed his vocation despite severe and continual problems. The physical problems, though great, were always minor compared to problems with those who were against him and his work.

And third, although Francis was very successful in converting thousands to Christ, he remembered that it was God who produced the results of his ministry. We do the work, but God produces what he wants from our work. Thus, if we are living our vocations to the best of our abilities, we should never take credit for the fruits of our labors, nor should we beat ourselves up when our work seems to produce very little.

And that is the good news I have for you on this Ascension Sunday.

Story source: "St. Francis Xavier," in *Butler's Lives of the Saints: December – New Full Edition,* Revised by Kathleen Jones, 1999, Collegeville, Minnesota, Burns & Oates, The Liturgical Press, pp. 25-30.

Chapter 22

Pentecost - A
Hi Handsome, My Name Is Rose

Scripture:

- Acts of the Apostles 2: 1-11
- Psalm 104: 1ab & 24ac, 29bc-30, 31 & 34
- 1 Corinthians 12: 3b-7, 12-13
- John 20: 19-23

This Sunday, Catholic Christians throughout the world celebrate the Feast of Pentecost, the birthday of the Catholic Church in particular and Christianity in general. We see this as the birthday of the Church because it was on Pentecost that the Holy Spirit descended on the early disciples and bought them many gifts to go out to be missionaries to the world. Enthusiasm, courage, wisdom, and knowledge were just some of the gifts the Spirit brought. Unlike Judaism, which was insular and exclusive, the new religion was to be missionary and inclusive.

We, too, receive the Holy Spirit at our baptism. At our baptism we become temples of the Holy Spirit who dwells in our hearts. We become part of the priesthood of all believers, part of the living and dynamic Body of Christ. The Spirit comes again, of course, in Confirmation, a sacrament we'll celebrate at many of the Masses this weekend.

All of the gifts of the Spirit, from my perspective, are social in nature. That means that we are to share them with others. But the gifts of the Spirit must be exercised and cherished, for just like a muscle that will atrophy and wither if it is not used, so will our gifts. That means that every day, in every way, we need to counteract forces that may want us to give up, to get discouraged, to become less than joyful followers of Jesus.

In the following story, we can see how the Spirit operated in one woman's life. And, as a result, the light from the Spirit touched the hearts of all around her.

There was once a young man I'll call Joe who went to the local university to study. On the first day of class, the professor asked the students to get to know someone they didn't already know. As Joe stood up to look around, a gentle hand touched his shoulder. When he turned around, he found it was a little old lady with a radiant smile. She said, "Hi, handsome. My name is Rose. I'm eighty-seven. Can I give you a hug?"

Joe laughed and enthusiastically said, "Of course you may!" And she gave him a big hug.

"Why are you in college at your age?" Joe asked.

Rose jokingly said, "I'm here to find a rich husband, get married, and have a couple of kids…"

Joe said, "No, seriously. I'm curious why you're in college at the age of eighty-seven."

Rose replied, "I have always dreamed of having a college education, and now I'm getting one!"

After class, Rose and Joe went to the Student Union to get a milkshake and talk. They became instant friends. And for the rest of the semester, Joe and Rose would leave class together and talk nonstop. Joe was fascinated by Rose's wisdom and her stories.

Over the course of the year, Rose became quite the celebrity on campus and made friends easily wherever she went. She loved to dress up and revel in the attention the young students showered upon her. She was truly living it up.

At the end of the semester, the football team invited Rose to be the speaker at their annual banquet. As she walked up to the podium to give her prepared speech, Rose dropped her three-by-five cards on the floor on which she had written her notes.

Frustrated and embarrassed, she leaned into the microphone and said, "I'm sorry I'm so jittery. I gave up beer for Lent and this whiskey is killing me! I'll never get my speech cards back in order, so just let me tell you what I know."

After the laughter died down, Rose said, "We don't stop playing because we grow old; we grow old because we stop playing.

"There are just four things you need to stay young and be happy and achieve success. First, you have to laugh and find humor every day. Second, you need to have a dream. When you lose your dreams, you die. Many people walk around as though they are dead, for they don't have dreams.

"Third, remember that there is a difference between growing old and growing up. If you are nineteen and lie in bed for a full year and don't do one productive thing, you'll turn twenty. Anybody can grow older, for that doesn't take any talent or ability. The idea is to grow up by always finding opportunities to change. Have no regrets.

"And fourth, the elderly don't have regrets for what we did, but rather for the things we did not do. The only people who fear death are those with regrets."

When Rose finished her speech, she sang "The Rose" to the guests, and then she taught them the lyrics and challenged them to live them in their lives.

Rose went on to finish college and, one week after graduation, she died in her sleep. Two thousand college students came to the funeral of their dear old friend who had taught them, by her shining example of zestful living that it is never too late to be all they can be.

From looking at Rose's life, we see the Spirit at work. Joy, growth, humor, love, and tenderness radiated from Rose. And because of this, hearts were changed. This is truly a Pentecost story at its finest.

As we continue our life journeys this week, it would be good to ask ourselves how our lives radiate joy and enthusiasm and growth that shown so brightly in the life of Rose.

And that is the good news I have for you on this Pentecost Sunday.

Story source: Dan Clark, "Never Too Old to Live Your Dream," in Jack Canfield, Mark Victor Hansen, Kimberly Kirberger, and Dan Clark (Eds.), *Chicken Soup for the College Soul, Deerfield Park, Florida: Health Communications, Inc., 1999, pp. 290-291.*

Part Three

ORDINARY TIME

Chapter 23

Holy Trinity - A
Catherine of Sing Sing

Scripture:

- Exodus 34: 4b-6, 8-9
- Daniel 3: 52, 53, 54, 55
- 2 Corinthians 13: 11-13
- John 3: 16-18

This Sunday, Catholic Christians throughout the world celebrate the Feast of the Most Holy Trinity.

Though the concept of "Trinity" is not mentioned as such in the books of the Bible, most Christians believe in God the Father, God the Son, and God the Holy Spirit. This dogma holds that though there is only one God, there are three Divine Persons in this one God.

We see God the Father, who is often simply called "God," as the Creator of the Universe. We see God the Son, who came down to Earth and took a human form called Jesus, as our Redeemer or Savior. And we see God the Holy Spirit as the Sanctifier, Gift Giver, and Advocate (*Paraclete* in Greek).

In today's reading from St. Paul's Second Letter to the Corinthians, he says, "Brothers and sisters, rejoice. Mend your ways, encourage one another, agree with one another, live in peace, and the God of love and peace will be with you" (2 Corinthians 13: 11).

Though St. Paul was urging the early Christians to encourage one another, we should expand his advice to encourage everyone on their life journey. Everyone, from time to time, needs encouragement. Through encouragement, we can lighten others' burdens. That is what we see in the wonderful story, told by Tim Kimmel, about a woman named Catherine Lawes, a woman who would become known to many as "the warden's wife."

In 1921, Sing Sing Prison in New York State was known as one of the toughest prisons in the United States. That was the year when Lewis Lawes became the new warden.

Although Sing Sing had a notorious reputation for cruelty, by the time Lewis Lawes left the institution after serving their twenty years, it had become a more humanitarian place. Many people who study prisons attribute the changes to Lewis Lawes, but he insisted that the changes were due more to his wife than to himself. When people would give him credit for making the prison a more humane place, he would say, "I owe it all to my wonderful wife, Catherine, who is buried outside the prison walls."

Catherine was a mother with three young children when her husband, Lewis, became warden of Sing Sing. People warned her never to step inside the prison, for it was a very dangerous place. Catherine, however, did not listen to the people. When the first basketball game was held during Lewis' term, for example, Catherine insisted on attending the game with her children. She sat among the inmates.

Catherine would explain to critics, "My husband and I are going to take care of these men and I believe they will take care of me! I don't have to worry!"

Catherine also insisted on getting to know the men as people, not as prison numbers. For example, one day, she visited a blind man who had been convicted of murder. She took his hand in hers and asked if he read Braille. When he said he didn't know what Braille was, she taught him how. Years later, he wept for his love for her.

Another time, Catherine found a prisoner who was deaf-mute. So Catherine went to school to learn sign language, and then taught the prisoner. People said that from 1921 to 1937, Catherine made the body of Jesus come alive in Sing Sing Prison.

Then, one day, Catherine was killed in a car accident. The next morning, the warden didn't come to work. The whole prison knew that something was wrong.

The next day, Catherine's body lay in a casket at her home, three-quarters of a mile from the prison. The men gathered at the gate, tears streaming down their faces. The acting warden was shocked at the men's grief and sadness. Because he knew how much the men loved Catherine, he made a remarkable decision. He faced the men and said, "All right, men, you can go. Just be sure to check in tonight." He then opened the gate as the men of Sing Sing walked out, without any guards.

After walking the three-quarters of a mile to pay their respects to Catherine, they made their way back to Sing Sing. Every one of them returned.

The story of Catherine is not only inspirational. It is also a fine example of the power of encouragement in human lives.

To encourage means to inspire others with courage, spirit or confidence, or to promote someone's actions. Every human being, no matter how "together" and "problem-free" they may appear to be, needs to be encouraged from time to time. Encouragement is not just for children or for students or for young parents or for adults starting a new career or job. It is for everyone.

To encourage others on their life journeys is one way we can live the triple-love commandment of Jesus Christ. When we cheer another person on, we show our respect and our love for them.

As we continue our life journeys this week, it would be a good idea to reflect on our own lives. How do we encourage others? Who in our lives needs a bit of encouragement at this point in their lives?

And that is the good news I have for you on this Trinity Sunday.

Story source: Kimmel, Tim. "Changed Lives," in Gray, Alice (Ed.), *Stories for the Heart: 110 Stories to Encourage Your Soul,* Gresham, Oregon: Vision House Publishing, 1996, pp. 56-57.

Chapter 24

Holy Body and Blood of Christ – A
Babemba Peace Ritual

Scripture:

- Deuteronomy 8: 2-3, 14b-16a
- Psalm 147: 12-13, 14-15, 19-20
- 1 Corinthians 10: 16-17
- John 6: 51-58

Today the Catholic Church throughout the world celebrates the Feast of the Most Holy Body and Blood of Christ. In days gone by, this was called "Corpus Christi."

The feast comes to us from the Middle Ages and, in a sense, duplicates the focus of the Mass of the Lord's Supper on Holy Thursday. In other words, we celebrate the consecrated elements of the bread and wine that are turned into the Body and Blood of Christ at Eucharist or Mass.

But why is this important to Catholic Christians? After all, Jesus Christ is already really present in three other ways at Eucharist long before the bread and wine are consecrated: He is in the celebrant, in the proclaimed word, and in the assembly.

This fourth way Jesus is really present in the Eucharist is important to us because it is a special gift that Jesus gave us at the original Mass, the Last Supper. He commanded his followers to take his Body, in the element of bread, and eat it. He commanded his followers to take his Blood, in the element of wine, and drink it. And he commanded his followers to continue this ritual.

For two thousand years, now, Catholic Christians, through bishops and priests, have continued to follow Jesus' commands, and we treasure Holy Communion very much. In fact, we call the consecrated Host "The Blessed Sacrament" and make it the focus of our sanctuaries.

But this feast should also remind us that we are to be changed as a result of our contact with Jesus in the Eucharist and in Communion. We should not simply go to church, participate in the rituals, and then leave the same way we entered. On the contrary, we should become more in harmony with those around us. We should become holier and more generous. We should have our hearts softened. We should discard the pettiness or anger or hostilities that we may be harboring in our hearts. In short, Eucharist and Communion should help us to be reconciled to the Christ who lives in every one of us.

In some cultures, reconciliation is ritualized in customs outside of the Mass itself. That is what we can see in the amazing tribal ritual of the Babemba tribe of South Africa.

In that tribe, antisocial or criminal behavior is very rare. However, when it does occur, the tribe has a very interesting way of dealing with it.

The member who has acted irresponsibly is placed in the center of the village. All work stops and everyone in the village gathers around the guilty one in a large circle. Then, one at a time, all individuals, including the children, call out all the good things the person in the center of the circle has done in his or her lifetime.

Every good deed is remembered. Every strength and kind act is recited with reverence. All the guilty party's positive attributes are listed. None of the villagers are permitted to tell lies or to exaggerate or to be facetious. Sometimes this ceremony can last several days and doesn't stop until every villager is drained of every positive comment he or she can think of about the person in the middle of the circle.

During the ritual, not a single word of criticism about the guilty party or his or her irresponsible behavior is permitted. At the end of the ritual, the tribal circle breaks up, a joyful celebration begins, and the guilty party is welcomed back into the tribe.

The power of the overwhelming, positive influence strengthens the self-esteem of the accused person and makes him or her live up to expectations of the tribe. For this reason, this tribal ritual does not have to be performed very often.

It would be very interesting to see how this custom would work to resolve work or family conflicts.

In the Eucharist, we come together to share in the mystical celebration of Holy Thursday, Good Friday, and Easter Sunday. We do not re-enact these mysteries at Eucharist. Rather, in a mystical way, we actually enter the one and only passion, death and resurrection of Jesus.

So what should we learn from all of this?

First, we should be thankful for the precious gift that Jesus gave us, the gift of Eucharist and of Holy Communion. Often we take Eucharist or Mass for granted because we have plenty of priests in this country. We must be mindful that in some parts of the world the Eucharist is vanishing because there are not enough ordained priests.

Second, we should renew our commitment to follow Jesus' command to "take and eat" and "take and drink." He did not give us his precious Body and Blood to stare at it or lock it up in a box. He commanded us to eat it and drink it. That commandment is clear. Therefore, if there is a reason we are not following this commandment, we should investigate how to knock down the barrier so we may follow Jesus' command.

And third, we should remember that by receiving Communion at Eucharist, we should become changed. We should become more forgiving of others, more welcoming. We should be more generous with the gifts that God gave us. We should become better people.

And that is the good news I have for you on this Feast of the Most Holy Body and Blood of Christ.

Story source: Anonymous, "Tribal Ritual for Antisocial Behavior," in Brian Cavanaugh's *Sower's Seeds of Encouragement: Fifth Planting*, 1998, #92, p. 83.

Chapter 25

2nd Sunday in Ordinary Time - A
Thorns Into Flowers

Scripture:

- Isaiah 49: 3, 5-6
- Psalm 40: 2 & 4ab, 7-8a, 8b-9, 10
- 1 Corinthians 1: 1-3
- John 1: 29-34

Today we begin the season of the Church Year known as Ordinary Time. This season celebrates the life of Christ in general, rather than focusing on a specific aspect of his life as we do during the Christmas or Easter Seasons. Ordinary time is named after ordinal numbers (such as First, Second, Third) because those are how the Sundays and weeks of Ordinary Time are named.

It is fitting that we begin Ordinary Time by hearing about the Baptism of Jesus. As we mentioned last week, baptism is what makes us Christians, members of the Body of Christ on Earth. At our baptism, we become anointed ministers of the Church and receive many graces as well as many responsibilities.

One of the things that we often overlook when we discuss baptism, though, is that we become one with Christ's suffering, not just his glory. In fact, we hear that we "die with Christ" at our baptism. That means our old self is gone, and we are reborn into a new life of grace.

It also means that just as Christ suffered on Earth, we too are called as his followers to suffer also. Fortunately, however, suffering and death are not the last word for the Christian. Rather, they are states that lead to glory and everlasting life.

If you get older, you will realize that suffering is not the final word for the Christian. That is what we see in the following legend.

According to the story, there was once a monk who liked to walk in the monastery's gardens and reflect on spiritual things. One day, right before the beginning of Holy Week, he was walking alone in the gardens thinking about how Jesus suffered for us. Suddenly he saw a crown of thorns lying on the path. He imagined that the crown must have been similar to the crown of thorns Jesus must have worn when he was crucified.

The monk gently picked up the crown of thorns and placed it on the altar in the little chapel where the monks had Mass each day. The crown of thorns had a good effect on the other monks, for it made Jesus' suffering so much more real.

At last, Easter Sunday morning came. When the monks came into the little chapel to say their morning prayers, they were all astonished to see that the crown of thorns, lit up by the sunshine coming through the windows, was now quite different. All of the thorns had turned into beautiful flowers.

As they gazed at the crown of flowers, they reflected that it is from suffering and sacrifice that the greatest spiritual fruits are produced.

This is a beautiful legend indeed, for it captures the good news of Catholic Christianity. Here are just three things we can learn.

First, suffering can produce great spiritual growth in a person. If you live long enough, you will see this over and over again. Many saints, for example, talk about their "dark night of the soul" or being in a spiritual desert. At those times, they suffer intensely. Their prayer life seems to be dry and without fruit. They are in the "bitter valley." The only thing that keeps them going is their faith, their belief that despite the intense struggles they are experiencing, the pain is not the last word. Rather, a loving God is watching over them and loving them and will one day give them rest. Saints such as John of the Cross and Mother Teresa talk about such pain in their writings.

Second, pain and suffering are part of the human condition. In history, we see that many peoples of the world interpreted suffering as God being angry with them or punishing them for something. This kind of thinking has led some religious groups to treat those in pain as "deserving" of their suffering and, therefore, deserving of being treated as inferior people. We see this in Hinduism, for example.

Other groups believe that sickness is something that God gives people because he hates them. In the fields of nursing and medicine, this is called the "primitive" view of illness.

Other groups, based on this idea, believe that if a person does something that leads to illness, they lose the right to be loved and given health care. For example, in recent years, there was a person in the North Carolina legislature who wanted to deny health care to people who got lung cancer from smoking. or obesity from overeating, or AIDS from intimacy. Nowhere, of course, does Jesus tell his followers to judge others to determine whether or not they "deserve" love. We Christians are to love all people.

Finally, although suffering can lead the individual to spiritual growth, Jesus gave us a wise warning not to go looking for trouble. While lecturing his disciples about the folly of worry, he said, "Do not worry about tomorrow; tomorrow will take care of itself. Sufficient for a day is its own evil" (Matthew 6: 34). In other words, there is plenty of trouble in our lives without deliberately going to look for it.

As we continue our life journey this week, it would be a good idea to examine the sorrows in our lives. What kinds of suffering do we experience? How do they help us grow? What painful times in our lives led to great spiritual awareness and growth?

And that is the good news I have for you on this Second Sunday in Ordinary Time.

Story source: "The Crown of Thorns" by M.C.C. in Anthony Castle's, *A Treasury of Quips, Quotes, &Anecdotes for Preachers and Teachers*, 1998, p. 348.

Chapter 26

3rd Sunday in Ordinary Time - A
St. Francis de Sales

Scripture:

- Isaiah 8: 23 - 9: 3
- Psalm 27: 1, 4, 13-14
- 1 Corinthians 1: 10-13, 17
- Matthew 4: 12-23

As we gather to celebrate the Eucharist on this Third Sunday in Ordinary Time, we hear how Jesus called four fishermen to follow him as apostles: Peter, his brother Andrew, and James and John. Immediately they left their nets and followed the Lord.

Such vocation stories are always inspirational, for they show a profound faith, a kind of faith that a small child might place in a parent. From reading vocational stories, we can always glean some insights that we can apply in our own lives, for every one of us has a calling or vocation.

Some, like Francis de Sales, have more than one calling. Francis de Sales lived from 1567-1622, the son of a senator from Savoy in France. From an early age, Francis' father had great hopes and plans for his son, wanting the boy to grow up and follow in his footsteps. Therefore, Francis' father sent Francis first to Paris and then to Padua for studies.

After receiving his doctorate, Francis returned home. He was not satisfied, however, and felt that God was calling him to become a priest. Although his father fought Francis' desire, eventually Francis won him over and was ordained a priest of the Diocese of Geneva.

Geneva, at this time, was a hotbed of Calvinism. Calvinism, a branch of Protestant Christianity, is best known for its teachings on predestination.

When he was just 35 years old, Francis was consecrated as Bishop of Geneva. Though he was an administrator, he never lost his touch as a very pastoral priest. As a result of his pastoral sensitivity, he won many souls. He held that one could catch more flies with a spoonful of honey than with a barrelful of vinegar.

Francis de Sales, in addition to his administrative works as a bishop and pastoral duties as a priest, found time to write. He is best known for two books, *A Treatise on the Love of God* and *Introduction to the Devout Life*. He also wrote many pamphlets explaining the basics of the Catholic faith. These writings converted many people to Catholic Christianity, and he was such an effective writer that he has been named a patron saint of writers, journalists, and the Catholic Press.

Francis also contributed much to the field of vocations. He insisted, for example, that one can be a saint no matter what their role in life is. In *Introduction to the Devout Life*, Francis wrote, "It is an error, or rather a heresy, to say devotion is incompatible with the life of a soldier, a tradesman, a prince, or a married woman.... It has happened that many have lost perfection in the desert who had preserved it in the world."

Along with St. Jane Frances de Chantal, Francis founded the Sisters of the Visitation, also known as the Salesian Sisters.

Frances de Sales was canonized in 1664 and declared a Doctor (Teacher) of the Church in 1877 because of his insightful spiritual writing.

From looking at the life of St. Francis de Sales, at least three aspects of vocation come to mind.

First, even though our primary vocation or calling is to be a follower of Jesus Christ, how we live out that vocation can and often does change over time. In times past, many men, for example, stayed with one occupation and with one employer their whole working lives. Many women, too, stayed at home caring for the house and children their whole lives.

Today, however, people not only don't stay with one occupation their entire lives, they move to different localities and work for different companies. St. Francis de Sales, for example, started out as a lawyer, and then became a priest, then a bishop, and also a writer. His life shows how God can call us to different tasks at different points in our lives.

Second, how we live our vocations is shaped by the times and places in which we live. Often we don't reflect on why God chose us to live in this place at this point in history, even though it is always by divine design.

St. Francis de Sales, for example, lived in a time when there were many challenges to Catholic Christianity. God blessed Francis with the gift of writing, clarity of thought, pastoral sensitivity, and a passion for truth. Putting these all together, Francis spent much of his energy combating Calvinist thinking. If he had lived in another period of history, perhaps he would have used his talents to translate the Bible into another language or to fight against another false doctrine.

Finally, individuals *can* make a difference in the world. Though we value group efforts to solve problems, we should never forget the power that a single individual can exercise in the world. All we need to do is look at people like Gandhi, Martin Luther King, Jr., Mother Teresa, or hundreds of thousands of other world heroes.

As we continue our life journeys this week, it would be a good idea to examine our own vocational journeys. How is our path unfolding?

How is it changing and growing? What difference do we make in this world?

And that is the good news I have for you on this Third Sunday in Ordinary Time.

Story source: "St. Francis de Sales," in *Butler's Lives of the Saints: January – New Full Edition.* Collegeville, Minnesota: Burns & Oates, The Liturgical Press, Revised by Paul Burns, 1998, pp. 165-173.

Chapter 27

4th Sunday in Ordinary Time – A
Kuwaiti Resistance

Scripture]:

- Zephaniah 2: 3; 3: 12-13
- Psalm 146: 6c-7, 8-9a, 9bc-10
- 1 Corinthians 1: 26-31
- Matthew 5: 1-12a

As we gather to celebrate the Eucharist today, we encounter the famous passage from St. Matthew called "The Beatitudes." In this passage, Jesus gives us great insights into the kind of people he treasures.

Although there are many aspects of the Beatitudes that we could explore, today I want to explore the concept of being "poor in spirit."

Being "poor in spirit" refers to being detached from the things of the world, recognizing that we do not actually "own" material things. Rather, God owns this entire world and all its riches. We merely use the things of the world and share what we have with others. In other words, we are merely stewards of the material world.

All of us could list many ways that we have seen good stewardship in action in our lives. Today I give you another example that comes from the country of Kuwait in the Middle East.

In 1990, Iraq invaded the little neighboring country of Kuwait. During the time the Iraqis occupied Kuwait, the people of Kuwait suffered a great deal. There were killings and torture and looting of the shops. There was also much hunger because the people were afraid to leave their homes to go to the store, and there were food shortages.

But whenever we see tragedy in the world, we also see the human spirit rising to overcome the tragedy. In Kuwait, it was the Kuwaiti resistance that showed the human spirit at its best.

The Kuwaiti resistance did not involve guns or bombs or violence. Rather, it involved good stewardship. This is how the resistance worked. Each week, resistance workers would gather in a secret place and collect sugar, rice, and other food staples from underground food suppliers. At night, or early in the morning, the resistance workers would fan out to different parts of their cities delivering food to special homes called "main stores." Each of these homes would then be responsible for delivering the food to nine neighboring homes.

The resistance workers also helped the people with money, but that money had to be given anonymously. Therefore, if a well-off family knew of a family that needed money, they would put money in an envelope and slip it under the door of the needy household early in the morning.

The Kuwaiti resistance showed that through sacrifice and generosity, they were able to resist the evil that had visited them with the Iraqi occupation.

In this story, we see how the Kuwaiti people put the concept of being "poor in spirit" into action. From this story, and from the reflections of many Catholic thinkers through the centuries, we can make certain observations of "poverty of spirit."

Being poor in spirit means we recognize that all we have is a gift from God. Therefore, we are to thank God for our blessings. We are to develop the blessings he gives us and share them abundantly with others. And finally, we are to give back to the Lord the "first fruits" of our riches. "First fruits" means "off the top." Giving ten percent of our time, talent, and treasure is known as "tithing," for the root word of "tithe" is "ten."

Catholic Christians often do not tithe. Rather, they give much less than ten percent to the Lord. Regardless of how much we give to the Lord, though, we are called to challenge ourselves so that one day we can truly say we tithe as the Bible asks of us.

Each year at this time, Catholic Christians in many dioceses are asked to give in a special way to the third level of Church—the diocese. In case you may have forgotten, there are four levels of Church on Earth. The first level is called the home or the "domestic church." Parents, who are part of the "priesthood of all believers," head it. The second level is called "the parish," in which Catholic Christians live out their faith in community and celebrate the milestones of their lives. An ordained priest heads it. All Catholic Christians are asked to be registered and active members of a parish. The third level of Church is called the diocese, headed by a bishop. And the fourth level of Church on Earth is called the Universal Church and is headed by the Bishop of Rome, also known as the pope.

Today we are asked to make a pledge to the Bishop's Annual Appeal (BAA). The appeal supports many essential ministries carried on at the Diocesan level, such as campus ministry, seminarian education, Catholic schools, Hispanic ministry, marriage counseling, and many more.

We know that when we make a pledge over time, we can afford more than when we try to give money all at once. Just I did last year, I challenge you to pledge the cost of a $13.50 pizza per week. Over the 26 weeks of the campaign, that would come out to $350 or $58 per month. As always, I will give triple of what I ask of you. For those who can give more, please be generous.

Our parish is noted for its generous people, and that is why we always make our BAA goal. I'm confident we will rise to the challenge of this year's goal.

And that is the good news I have for you on this Fourth Sunday in Ordinary Time.

Story source: "Becoming a Community" by Anonymous. In Brian Cavanaugh's *Sower's Seeds of Encouragement; Fifth Planting,* 1998, #20, pp. 19-20.

Chapter 28

5th Sunday in Ordinary Time – A
The Light of Ben Shaw

Scripture:

- Isaiah 58: 7-10
- Psalm 112: 4-5. 6-7. 8a & 9
- 1 Corinthians 2: 1-5
- Matthew 5: 13-16

As we gather to celebrate the Eucharist on this Fifth Sunday in Ordinary Time, we are challenged to put our faith into action, to be "lights to the world."

In the following story, we see how one man followed the Lord by being a light to the world and, as a result, showed others how to live.

There was once a man I'll call "Pete" who lay desperately ill on a motel floor in a southern city. Pete was an alcoholic who had not had a drink for some time and was about to go into convulsions as a result. He was able to crawl to a telephone and ask the operator to call Alcoholics Anonymous for him. He was trembling too much to dial the phone himself.

Within ten minutes, a man named Ben Shaw walked through the door and treated Pete with incredible reverence. He brought Pete to a hospital detoxification center to begin the painful process of alcoholic withdrawal.

As Pete began his recovery, he was filled with shame and guilt and remorse and humiliation. Ben Shaw, a fallen-away Catholic Christian, continued to nurture Pete. He told Pete that God loved him and cared for him and was watching over him. Ben told Pete that alcoholism was a disease, not a sin. He was sick person needing to get well, not bad person needing to become good.

Ben gave Pete some literature from the American Medical Association that talked about alcoholism as a biological-psychological disease. Ben told Pete he should no more be ashamed about his alcoholism than someone with diabetes or cancer should be ashamed of their disease. Above all else, Ben told Pete that he cared for him and so did God. In fact, Ben said, when God's children fall, he does not scold them. Rather, God scoops them up and comforts them.

As Pete's recovery allowed him to think more clearly, he learned that Ben Shaw was a recovering alcoholic, and that he was an itinerant laborer who showed up at Manpower each day. Although Ben had to put cardboard in his shoes to cover the holes, Ben went out and bought Pete a meal from McDonald's when he was ready to eat, and stayed with him a full week. Ben breathed life into Pete and never asked for a thing in return.

Pete later learned that Ben Shaw had lost his family and fortune through drinking, and that at night he would sometimes be so lonely that he would talk to his television hoping that it would talk back to him. Each night before going to sleep, Ben would spend fifteen minutes reading a meditation book and thank God for his mercy.

Pete eventually recovered and became a priest. He lost touch with Ben Shaw. Pete never did, however, forget Ben Shaw and his tremendous kindness.

Then, two years after his ordination, Pete returned to the same southern city where he had gotten sober. He went looking for Ben Shaw to reconnect and thank him for what he had done for him two years earlier. Pete learned that Ben Shaw had gone back to drinking and was now living on Skid Row.

Pete went to Skid Row searching for Ben Shaw, and for a moment he thought he saw Ben sitting in a doorway. When he bent down to greet the man, however, he realized it was not Ben but a pathetic alcoholic who asked for a dollar to get some wine. Pete, or rather I should say "Father Pete," took the suffering alcoholic's hands in his and kissed them. The wino had tears in his eyes, for more than money, he craved love and acceptance. Fr. Pete remembered what Mother Teresa of Calcutta had said, that the greatest pain was the feeling of not being accepted or wanted.

Several days later, while Fr. Pete was celebrating Mass for a group of recovering alcoholics, he saw Ben Shaw enter the church. Unfortunately, though, Ben Shaw disappeared during the distribution of Communion.

Two days later, though, Fr. Pete received a letter from Ben Shaw. Ben told Fr. Pete that he had been on Skid Row the day Pete was looking for him, and he had seen Fr. Pete kiss the hands of the suffering alcoholic on the sidewalk. He told Fr. Pete that because of his action, he had thrown away his bottle and was now making another attempt at sobriety. He told Fr. Pete that his kindness released him from the shadow world of panic. Ben Shaw ended his letter by saying, "Fr. Pete, if you should ever wonder who Ben Shaw is, remember I am someone you know very well. I am every man and woman you meet."

What a beautiful story this is, for it shows how powerful being a light to the world really is.

As Catholic Christians, we are called to be lights to the world. That means we are to put our faith into action. Jesus told us that when we stand before him, he would hold us responsible for what we did for the "least of our brethren."

He did not say we would be quizzed on abstract doctrines or whether we can list the names of the Apostles or rattle off the books of the Bible in chronological order. He did not say we would be excused from *doing* our faith just because we accepted him as our personal savior. He did say we would be judged on how we put our faith into action, not how we talked about it.

As we continue our life journeys, it would be a good idea to reflect on how we put our faith into action by serving those in need in our parish, our diocese, and our world.

And that is the good news I have for you on this Fifth Sunday in Ordinary Time.

Story source: "Ben Shaw" in William J. Bausch, *A World of Stories for Preachers and Teachers,* Mystic, CT: Twenty-Third Publications, 1998, pp. 167-169.

Chapter 29

6th Sunday in Ordinary Time
Integrity

Scripture:

- Sirach 15: 15-20
- Psalm 119: 1-2, 4-5, 17-18, 33-34
- 1 Corinthians 2: 6-10
- Matthew 5: 17-37

As we gather to celebrate the Eucharist on this Sixth Sunday in Ordinary Time, we encounter a wide variety of themes in the Scripture selections. We hear about God's wisdom; the call of Christians to righteousness; anger; reconciliation; adultery; lust; divorce; remarriage; oaths; and other subjects. Today I will talk about a virtue that we often neglect to discuss: Integrity.

In the Gospel reading, Jesus makes a profound statement when he says, "Let your 'Yes' mean 'Yes,' and your 'No' mean 'No.' Anything more is from the evil one" (Matthew 5: 37). What Jesus was talking about in this saying is part of the virtue of integrity.

Integrity refers to something being whole or complete. When it refers to human beings, integrity refers to the quality of being of sound moral principle. When we say someone is a person of integrity, we often say the person "has character."

The following anonymous essay, called "Needed: Men and Women of Character," lists some of the characteristics of the person of integrity.

"Needed: Men and Women of Character"
The world needs men and women…
who cannot be bought;
whose word is their bond;
who put character above wealth;
who possess opinions and a strong will;
who are larger than their vocations;
who do not hesitate to take risks;
who will not lose their individuality in a crowd;
who will be as honest in small affairs as in greater;
who will make no compromise with wrong;
whose ambitions are not confined to their own selfish desires;
who will not say they do it "because everybody else does it";
who are true to their friends through good and bad, in adversity as well as in prosperity;
who do not believe that shrewdness, cunning, and hardheadedness are the best qualities for winning success;

who are not ashamed or afraid to stand for the truth
when it is unpopular;
who can say "no" with emphasis, although all the rest
of the world says "yes."

This essay speaks to all of us, for I believe that deep in our hearts, we all want to be people of character, people of integrity. Sometimes we fail, but if we are truly people of integrity, we overwhelmingly live our lives to reflect that integrity.

Although there are many dimensions to this virtue, here are three principles that we can use in our lives to keep us on track.

First, we must let our word be our bond. In times past, people often did not need to use lawyers as much as they do today. A handshake was considered as good as gold; it was a person's bond. If two people made a deal, a handshake meant it would happen.

In parish life, there are many people whose word is their bond. When they say they are going to do something, it will happen. If, for some reason they can't accomplish what they said they would do, they let others know. Pastors, of course, treasure such people, for they are worth their weight in gold!

Second, though we should stick with our principles, we should always have an open mind. It is just possible that we don't know everything. When I was little, my father told me, "Son, when you find yourself going in a direction opposite everyone else, it is a good idea to take some time to re-examine your ideas. You just might be wrong." That has always been excellent advice, for there is a huge difference between having strong principles and being closed-minded or bullheaded.

In parish life, for example, there are often people who have what they believe are very fine ideas, and they want to share these ideas with the community. Unfortunately, though, they do not always see the full picture. Thus, their plans are incomplete and their behavior can steer others in wrong directions. There are important bits of information that the pastor may know, for example, that they don't know. Thus, we always need to be aware that there might be more to the situation than meets the eye.

And third, people of integrity must always remember that charity is the supreme virtue. St. John XXIII summed this principle up by saying,

"In essentials, unity; in non-essentials, liberty; in all things, charity." St. Augustine, several centuries before him, said pretty much the same thing.

What John XXIII was saying, was that Catholic Christians need to distinguish between "essentials" of the Faith and "non-essentials." "Essentials" of the Faith include unchangeable beliefs such as there is One God but Three Divine Persons in One God. "Non-essentials" of the Faith include such things as belief in saintly apparitions. With non-essentials of the Faith, we should have the liberty or freedom to believe, not believe, or doubt. But no matter what our opinions or beliefs about the non-essentials of the Faith, we should always put charity in practice. In other words, we are to treat others as we treat Christ. That is, after all, what a person of integrity would do.

As we continue our life journey this week, it would be a good idea to reflect on how we are people of integrity and how we sometimes fail to be people of integrity.

And that is the good news I have for you on this Sixth Sunday in Ordinary Time.

Story source: Anonymous, "Needed: Men and Women of Character," in Brian Cavanaugh's *Sower's Seeds that Nurture Family Values: Sixth Planting,* 2000, #37, p. 46.

Chapter 30

7th Sunday in Ordinary Time – A
Love Your Enemies

Scripture:

- Leviticus 19: 1-2, 17-18
- Psalm 103: 1-2, 3-4, 8 & 10, 12-13
- 1 Corinthians 3: 16-23
- Matthew 5: 38-48

As we gather to celebrate the Eucharist on this Seventh Sunday in Ordinary Time, we hear Jesus talk to his disciples about love. Instead of hating one's enemies, we are to love them and pray for them. And if anyone harms us, we are to "offer no resistance."

Needless to say, this teaching of Jesus was pretty radical for the people of his day. They were used to holding to such Biblical injunctions as "An eye for an eye and a tooth for a tooth." They were used to the idea of loving one's friends and hating one's enemies. But Jesus, as he usually did, commanded the opposite of conventional wisdom.

In today's world, the word "enemies" could refer to anyone whom we find troublesome or problematic. Although we know we are to find Christ in human beings and treat them accordingly, each of us sometimes fails. That is what happened to the minister in the following story by Fr. Jim McNamara.

There was once a young minister who was called to his office to see a young man. It was almost suppertime, and the minister was not pleased to be called to his office because it was his day off.

When he got to his office, he found a young man. His clothes were dirty, and he smelled terrible. The minister correctly identified him as a street person. The young man introduced himself only as "Jim." As Jim began to tell his story, he told the minister that he had no place to stay.

The minister immediately suspected that the young man was going to ask him for money. Deep inside himself, he hoped that his housekeeper would interrupt him and call him to dinner. The young man continued with his very sad story. The minister felt the story dragging on and on, and occasionally glanced at his watch.

During the young man's story, the housekeeper interrupted to tell the minister that he had a phone call. He excused himself and went to answer the phone in another room.

When the minister returned to his office, he found that the young man had left. The minister realized that his manner and lack of compassion probably made the young man feel less than welcome. Therefore, he went to the door and looked up and down the street to see if he could find the young man, but he could not see the departed visitor. Feeling remorseful for the insensitive way he had treated the young man, he got in his car and went through the neighborhood looking for the young man.

Finally he spotted Jim and pulled his car to the curb. When he called out, Jim just kept on walking. So, the minister parked his car, ran up the sidewalk, and stood in front of the young man. "Jim, I'm sorry that I had to leave. Would you come back with me and finish our conversation?"

The young man just shrugged and said in a low voice, "You're just like everybody else. No one wants to listen." With that, Jim walked around the minister and disappeared into the night.

What a sad story this is. What makes it even sadder is the every one of us, at one time or another, has treated others in a way that is insensitive or lacks compassion. We failed to see Christ who lived in the person, the Christ who called out for kindness and understanding.

Reflecting on Jesus' command to love those we don't particularly like, we need to keep several things in mind. Here are just three of the principles we should consider.

First, it is a good idea to identify the types of people that we have trouble accepting in a kind and sensitive way. In the world of hospitals, a world in which I have worked most of my life, I know that there are certain types of patients that staff members have a difficult time accepting. These include patients who are demanding and ungrateful, or loud and rude, or who have problems that they brought on themselves. In everyday life, each of us has certain people whom we don't like: the constant complainer who does nothing to change their life circumstance; the whiner; the lazy person; the self-righteous person who thinks they're holier than everyone else; the know-it-all; the busybody; the gossiper; the judgmental person; and so on.

Second, once we know what types of people we have trouble accepting, we can take measures to be especially careful to be kind and sensitive to such persons. People who work in customer service have to do this as a matter of course every day. In our own lives, maybe we have an in-law who knows how to "push our buttons." When they come to our homes for a visit, we can make a plan for how to reduce the possibility that we will treat them in the same way they are treating us. This of course takes great maturity, both emotionally and spiritually.

And finally, though we are to see Christ in every person, there are times when we need to put the needs of the group ahead of the needs of the individual. This happens in organizations all the time. When a person is destroying the family unit because of an addiction-related negative behavior, for example, we need to remember that the good of the group may trump the needs of the individual.

As we continue our life journeys this week, it would be a good idea to reflect on what kind of people we have the hardest time accepting as Christ. How do we try to accept them kindly? Have we ever had to ban people from a group for which we are responsible because they were having a negative effect on the group?

And that is the good news I have for you on this Seventh Sunday in Ordinary Time.

Story source: "Power of Compassion" by Fr. Jim McNamara. In Brian Cavanaugh's *More Sower's Seeds: Second Planting,* 1992, #62, pp. 59-60.

Chapter 31

8th Sunday in Ordinary Time - B
Worry and 21 Words

Scripture:

- Isaiah 49: 14-15
- Psalm 62: 2-3, 6-7, 8-9ab
- 1 Corinthians 4: 1-5
- Matthew 6: 24-34

As we gather to celebrate the Eucharist on this Eighth Sunday in Ordinary Time, we hear Jesus telling us that we should not worry about tomorrow, for God is watching over us.

Worry, though, is something every one of us experiences. We worry about bills and our health. We might be worried about our safety from the classroom bully. We may worry about our jobs and our future. We worry about who will be elected, our adult children, and a variety of other things.

One man who worried a great deal was Sir William Osler. In 1871, young William was studying to become a physician. He was worried about passing his final exam. He was worried about what he would do if he did pass his exam, and where he would go, and how he would build up a medical practice, and how he would make a living. In short, he worried about the future.

Then, one day, he picked up a book and read twenty-one words that changed his life. These words, written by nineteenth-century writer Thomas Carlyle, were: "Our main business is not to see what lies dimly at a distance, but to do what lies clearly at hand." In other words, focus on what needs doing today, not on what may need doing tomorrow.

Young William followed the advice of Thomas Carlyle. He decided to focus each day on that day, not on the following day. As a result, he began to worry less about the future, and because he spent his energy on the tasks at hand, he was able to become one of the most famous physicians of his time. He was even made a knight by the King of England, and two huge volumes containing 1,466 pages were required to tell the story of his amazing life.

Worry, in the context that Jesus was talking about it, refers to feeling distressed, anxious, uneasy, or troubled. It specifically refers to thinking that something bad might happen in the future.

If we insist on worrying, there is a technique from the world of psychiatric-mental health nursing that is often very effective. It is called "packaging." We "package" our worry into a fifteen-minute session per 24 hours—say 10 a.m.-10:15 a.m. When we find ourselves worrying about a specific situation, and it's 2 p.m., we say, "No, it's not time for the worry; that's scheduled for 10 a.m. tomorrow." Then we can put the worry out of our mind and focus on the now.

Worry is a difficult concept to explore in just one homily because it is so pervasive in our lives and because there are so many types of worry. However, today I give just three points to consider when worrying about the future.

First, remember that each one of us has only one primary goal: to become a saint. When we realize that, everything else is put in perspective. That means that our ultimate goal is not to have perfect health in this life. Our ultimate goal is not to possess the things of this world. Our ultimate goal is not to achieve bliss in this life. Our ultimate goal is to get to heaven one day.

Second, most worry is about the future. Therefore, as Jesus told his followers, and as Sir William Osler found, we should focus on living our lives today. In other words, we should live our vocations as best we can. Like St. Therese, the "Little Flower", we are to do everyday tasks as well as we possibly can to give glory to God. We are to get into life with full gusto.

Oftentimes people live life half-heartedly. They do the minimum amount of work, cut corners whenever possible, and are lazy. Such people procrastinate and fail to complete what they set out to do. Because of how they live, their conscience never gives them peace. Rather, that little voice in the back of their heads is whispering, "You are a second-rate person. You are not worthy. You are inferior." As a result, such people rarely achieve serenity or peace in their lives.

Now some people, when they hear that they are supposed to focus on today instead of tomorrow, believe this means that they are supposed to avoid planning. This is faulty thinking. Planning for tomorrow is indeed a task of today. I repeat: *Planning for tomorrow is a task of today*. Planning is not the same as worrying. If a college student wants to become a teacher, for example, he or she needs to plan out a schedule of courses wisely. Otherwise, the student will not succeed. Most of us know we need to plan in advance, and we do it. We make a list before we go to the grocery store, for example, so that we don't forget to buy something we need. We put gas in the car today so we can go on our trip tomorrow. And because we have a plan we do not worry about the outcome.

Finally, when we are consumed with worry, we need to turn this worry over to God. Assuming that we have done all we can do, we then ask

God to give us peace. Maybe we might pray, "All right, God, I've had it. The burden I'm carrying is just too much. I can't handle it any more. Therefore, I'm giving it to you. My worry is so great that it is consuming me, and I can't focus on what I need to be focused on." Often, when I have prayed like this, I find an immediate relief.

As we continue our life journeys this week, it would be a good idea to explore how we handle worry. How do our worries stack up when we consider that our ultimate goal is to be a saint?

And that is the good news I have for you on this Eighth Sunday in Ordinary Time.

Story source: Anonymous, "Twenty-one Words to Change Your Life," in Brian Cavanaugh's *Sower's Seeds that Nurture Family Values: Sixth Planting,* 2000, #92, pp. 97-98.

Chapter 32

9th Sunday in Ordinary Time – A
The Job Applicant

Scripture:

- Deuteronomy 11: 18, 26-28, 32
- Psalm 31: 2-3a, 3bc-4, 17 & 25
- Romans 3: 21-25, 28
- Matthew 7: 21-27

As we gather to celebrate the Eucharist on this Ninth Sunday in Ordinary Time, we hear Jesus telling us that just as a house needs to be built on a firm foundation, we must create our lives on a firm foundation. If we don't do this, the storms of life will destroy us.

Now many people go through life in a scattered, haphazard fashion. They do not plan. They live beyond their means. They do not prepare for the future. They are not prudent in handling the things of the world for which they are responsible.

Frequently such people see life as something that is guided by "Lady Luck," an imaginary figure that guides their destiny. To them, when good things happen, it's a matter of "good luck," and when bad things happen, it's a matter of "bad luck." They fail to make the connection between their own behavior and the outcomes they experience.

Such people fail to realize that "luck" is almost always nothing more than the consequence of hard work and preparation. That is what the young men in the following story found out.

Before the 20th Century, the telegraph was the fastest method of communication for long-distance communication. Morse code, a system of dots and dashes put in various combinations to form letters, was the way the system worked. Naturally, to be a telegraph operator, a person had to be an expert in Morse code, both in sending it and hearing it.

One day, a young man read a newspaper ad about an opening for a Morse code operator. Immediately he went to the telegraph agency to apply for the job. When he arrived at the office, he encountered a busy office filled with noise and the sound of a telegraph in the background. The sign on the receptionist's counter instructed applicants to fill out an application form and wait until they were asked to come into the inner office.

The young man took a form and sat down with several other young men who had been waiting since before he arrived. After a few minutes, the young man got up and walked into the inner office. The other applicants were curious why this young man went into the office without being called.

Within a couple of minutes, though, the employer escorted the young man into the waiting room and said, "Gentlemen, thank you very much for coming, but this young man has been hired."

The other applicants began to grumble, and one spoke up saying, "Wait a minute. Why was this guy hired? We were here before he was! We didn't even get to be interviewed, yet he got the job!"

The employer said, "I'm sorry, but all the time you have been sitting in this office, the telegraph has been ticking out the following message in Morse code: 'If you understand this message, then come right in. The job is yours.' None of you heard or understood it. This young man did. That is why the job is his."

What a wonderful story this is, for it shows that to be successful in life, we have to prepare correctly. In Jesus' terms, we need to build a house on solid foundation.

Here are three practical ideas on how we can build a solid life.

First, we need to remember that there is no such thing as "Lady Luck" who guides our lives. God guides our lives.

Second, although God guides our lives, he does not run our lives. He gives us certain talents, puts us in a certain time and place, surrounds us with certain opportunities, and then lets us work. With this knowledge, we thank God for all the talents he has given us. We then work hard to develop our talents, such as by going to school to prepare for a career. We then put these developed gifts into action by sharing the fruits of the gifts with others. And finally we give back to the Lord the first fruits of our labor. In the biblical context, this is called tithing, or giving the first ten percent of what we earn to the Lord.

And third, we build a solid life when we use common sense in living our lives. As people living in the United States at the beginning of the 21st Century, this means certain things. For example, building a solid life or a "house on a firm foundation" means that we save money. We live below our means, spending less than we bring in. It means always have a "Plan B" and a "Plan C" for events on our life journey in case our "Plan A" fails. It means being people of extraordinary generosity, realizing that the more generous we are towards others, the more generous God will be with us. It means adopting a pervasive spirit of gratitude, always focusing on what we have instead of what we don't have. And very importantly, it means treating everyone, as we would like to be treated. That is called building a house on a solid foundation.

As we continue our life journeys this week, it would be a good idea to ask ourselves how we have built a solid life or how we are failing to do so.

And that's the good news I have for you on this Ninth Sunday in Ordinary Time.

Story source: "The Job Applicant," by Mark Jevert, in Wayne Rice's *Hot Illustrations for Youth Talks*, 1993, pp. 126-127.

Chapter 33

10th Sunday in Ordinary Time - A
Sr. Mary Mercy, M.M.

Scripture:

- Hosea 6: 3-6
- Psalm 50: 1 & 8, 12-12, 14-15
- Romans 4: 18-25
- Matthew 9: 9-13

Today, Catholic Christians celebrate the Tenth Sunday in Ordinary Time.

In today's Gospel passage from Matthew, we hear, "As Jesus passed on from there, he saw a man named Matthew sitting at the customs post. He said to him, 'Follow me.' And he got up and followed him" (Matthew 9: 9).

Just as Jesus called Matthew to follow him, he calls each of us as Christians to follow him also. And although most people do not have the call to be a missionary in foreign lands as the apostles did, some people do. One of those people who clearly heard God's call to the missionary life, and who answered it, was a young woman named Elizabeth Josephine Hirschboeck.

Elizabeth was born on March 10, 1903 in Milwaukee, Wisconsin. She attended Catholic schools with her brothers. When she was nineteen years old, Elizabeth was traveling with a friend in a car driven by the friend's father. There was an accident, and Elizabeth's friend was killed. She took this as a sign from God that she should devote her life to Christ in a special way. She decided that she should be a medical doctor and a Religious Sister.

When Elizabeth wrote to Mother Mary Joseph of the Maryknoll Sisters, Mother Mary Joseph wrote back and encouraged Elizabeth to become a physician, and then apply to become a Sister. And that is exactly what Elizabeth did. After graduating from Marquette University School of Medicine in 1928, she entered Maryknoll in New York.

In those days, Maryknoll Sisters gave up their given name to take on a new name; hers was Sr. Mary Mercy. In 1931, Sr. Mercy found herself in Korea as a Maryknoll missionary. She did not speak Korean, and she did not have a license to practice medicine. She eventually secured the license, and set about to use her medical skills for the poor.

In those early years of her missionary work, Sr. Mercy gained the confidence of the people, not only with her medical skills, but also with her excellent sense of humor, compassion, patience, and common sense. She worked through bitterly cold winters and hot summers.

Sr. Mercy worked in Korea from 1931 to 1940. In 1940, she became seriously ill and returned to Maryknoll.

Three years later, in 1943, Sr. Mercy was well enough to begin working as a missionary physician in Riberalta, Bolivia. This jungle area is often called the "Green Hell" because of its intense, stifling heat, to say nothing of the ever-present snakes and crushing poverty.

When Sr. Mercy was in Riberalta, she was faced with an amazing amount of work in primitive conditions. The health statistics of the area showed 100% of the population with verminosis; 90% with amoebic dysentery; 60% with malaria; 30% with tuberculosis; and most with hookworm. Malnutrition was also the norm.

In *Hearts on Fire: The Story of the Maryknoll Sisters* by the late Penny Lernoux, we hear that to the Bolivians, Sr. Mercy was seen as an angel in white, while to visitors, she was seen as an angel of mercy in mud. A U.S. Public Health Service official said of Sr. Mercy, "My first, last and in-between recollections of Sister Mercy in Bolivia vary not a whit. I can still see her, plodding through mud, knee deep, the skirt of her otherwise white habit splattered and splashed, as she makes her way from hut to hut."

For seven years, Sr. Mercy worked in the jungles of Bolivia. Then, however, she heard about the many people forced to be refugees as a result of the Korean conflict. So she wrote to General Douglas MacArthur requesting that she be allowed to return to Korea to help. After being granted permission, she went to Pusan where she served thousands of refugees. For three and a half years, Sr. Mercy worked non-stop with refugees from the war until her health began to fail once again.

In 1954, Sr. Mercy left Korea to become the administrator of the Maryknoll Sisters' Queen of the World Hospital in Kansas City, Missouri. This hospital was the first integrated general hospital in the city, serving blacks and whites with equal dignity and respect.

In 1958, Sr. Mercy was elected Vicaress General of the Maryknoll Sisters. In 1973, she moved to the lower east side of New York City where she lived and worked with the poor of the city. She died on September 20, 1986.

When we look at the amazing life of Sr. Mercy, we cannot help but be inspired by her dedication, compassion, perseverance, and skill.

Though Sr. Mercy's life is certainly more movie-worthy than our own, we too are called to serve the Lord in our little corner of the world, day by day. Though we will probably never face the hardships that Sr. Mercy did in Korea or Bolivia, we too are called to serve God by serving others, especially those who are most in need. That is the missionary calling.

As we continue our life journeys this week, it would be a good idea to reflect on how we are living our missionary call.

And that is the good news I have for you on this Tenth Sunday in Ordinary Time.

Story source: "Mercy" in Penny Lernoux's *Hearts on Fire: The Story of the Maryknoll Sisters*, Maryknoll, N.Y.: Orbis Books, 1993, pp. 177-194.

Chapter 34

11th Sunday in Ordinary Time - A
San Pedro de San José Betancur

Scripture:

- Exodus 19: 2-6a
- Psalm 100: 1-2, 3, 5
- Romans 5: 6-11
- Matthew 9: 36 – 10: 8

Today, Catholic Christians celebrate the Eleventh Sunday in Ordinary Time.

On this day, we read in the Gospel of Matthew, "At the sight of the crowds, Jesus' heart was moved with pity for them because they were troubled and abandoned, like sheep without a shepherd. Then he said to his disciples, 'The harvest is abundant but the laborers are few; so ask the master of the harvest to send out laborers for his harvest'" (Matthew 9: 36-38). After he said that, Jesus sent out his disciples to work in the vineyard.

Through the centuries, there have been many priests who have, indeed, left their homeland to serve as missionaries in foreign lands. But not all missionaries have been priests. Some have been religious sisters or brothers or laypersons. Today we look at the life of a lay missionary who became the first canonized saint of Central America. His name is St. Pedro de San José Betancur.

Pedro was born in 1626 on the Island of Tenerife, the largest of the Canary Islands. His family was very poor. As a young man, Pedro worked as a shepherd in the Canary Islands.

When he was 24-years old, however, Pedro decided to journey to Guatemala where he had a relative who worked in government service. But by the time he got to Havana, Cuba, he was out of money. Therefore, he had to stay in Havana to work until he finally raised enough funds to go to Guatemala City.

After working many months in Cuba, Pedro finally arrived in Guatemala City, penniless. In fact, he was so poor that he ended up in a bread line that the Franciscan friars had in that city.

At this time, Pedro became convinced that God was calling him to become a priest. Therefore, he entered the local college run by the Jesuits to begin his priesthood studies. Unfortunately, however, poor Pedro was not able to master the material. As a result, he had to withdraw from the school.

In 1655, he joined the Secular Franciscan Order. It was in this lay state that he would serve the Church for the rest of his life.

Around 1658, Pedro began to do some very serious missionary work in Guatemala. Not only did he open a hospital for the poor, he also established a shelter for the homeless and a school for poor children. Pedro also had great compassion for prisoners, and he regularly visited them in their prison cells, giving them hope and a listening ear. He also spent time traveling the streets of Guatemala City inviting the richer residents to repent.

Other men of the town became attracted to Pedro and his work, and soon joined him. From this group came a religious community called the Hospitaller Bethlehemite (Belemite) Congregation, which was formally approved after his death.

Some people believe that that St. Pedro de San José Betancur was the original creator of the *posadas*, the nine-day celebration (December 16 – December 24) in which Joseph and Mary search for lodging. At the end of the search, they fine a *posada* or inn that will take them. This custom eventually spread to nations of Central America, South American, and in the North American countries of Mexico and the United States of America.

Pedro died in 1667.

On July 30, 2002, Pope John Paul II canonized Pedro in Guatemala City with a 500,000 people attending. The pope called him the "St. Francis of the Americas," and Pedro de San José Betancur became the first canonized saint of a Central American nation.

We cannot help but be inspired by reading the life of St. Pedro de San José Betancur, and we can learn many things from his life. Here are just three.

First, there is a powerful idea that when God closes one door, he opens another. Another way to look at this is to say: When God closes a door to us, it simply means that he has something much better in store for us behind another door. That is certainly what we see in Pedro's life. Though he thought God wanted him to be a priest, that door was closed to him. Perhaps his poor educational background did not provide a solid enough foundation. The important thing is that being rejected for priesthood studies did not sour Pedro's attitude or love of God and his Church. On the contrary, he found another way to serve.

Second, though not everyone is called to leave his or her homeland as St. Pedro de San José Betancur did, we are all called to serve those in need. This call to give drink to the thirsty, clothe the naked, visit the sick and imprisoned, and other works of mercy are Christian commandments that are for all Christians to follow, be they Catholic or not.

And third, though we often associate only priests or Religious Brothers or Sisters as missionaries, laypersons can be and are missionaries. In fact, in the United States, one of the largest and fastest-growing groups of Catholic missionaries is the Lay Maryknoll Missionaries (MKLM).

As we continue our life journeys this week, it would be a good idea to reflect on what kind of missionary work we do in our communities.

And that is the good news I have for you on this Eleventh Sunday in Ordinary Time.

___

Story sources:

- "St. Pedro de San José Betancur – Founder of the Hospitaller Bethlehemite (Belemite) Congregation." April 2015 – www.spreadjesus.org.
- "St. Pedro de San José Betancur." Saint of the Day, AmericanCatholic.org. April 2015.

Chapter 35

12th Sunday in Ordinary Time - A
Radiating Light

Scripture:

- Jeremiah 20: 10-13
- Psalm 69: 8-10, 14 & 17, 33-35
- Romans 5: 12-15
- Matthew 10: 26-33

Today, Catholic Christians celebrate the Twelfth Sunday in Ordinary Time.

In today's Gospel from Matthew, we hear Jesus tell his disciples not to be afraid of people who could harm their bodies. Specifically, he says, "Therefore do not be afraid of them. Nothing is concealed that will not be revealed, nor secret that will not be known. What I say to you in the darkness, speak in the light; what you hear whispered, proclaim on the housetops" (Matthew 10: 26-27).

In this teaching, Jesus is using the concept of light to indicate courage, truth, and goodness.

The concept of light is prominent in all world religions, including our own Christianity. In fact, there are festivals of light in Buddhism, Judaism, Islam, Hinduism, Paganism, and of course in Christianity. Christmas and Epiphany are the famous festivals of light for Christians.

In Catholic Christianity, the notion of light is used in many ways. For example, we often refer to Jesus as "the light" as in the phrase, "Christ, be our light." We also use the light of the sanctuary lamp to indicate that Jesus is present in the Blessed Sacrament. The light from the Easter candle is used at Baptism to indicate our faith. And the writers of the New Testament Scriptures, especially John, use the imagery of light to indicate understanding. People who live in darkness, on the other hand, do not understand Jesus and his message.

Even in life-after-life scientific research, we hear about "The Light." People from all over the world who have had a near-death experience, regardless of their religion or lack of it, report very much the same phenomenon of traveling down a long tunnel to "The Light."

One way light is used in religion is to describe people who radiate certain characteristics such as joy, love, and good humor. That is what we see in the following story called "Entertaining Royalty."

There were once a young man and woman who were walking in the Catskill Mountains in New York. As they walked along, they began talking about a young woman that they both knew.

The man said, "She has what I would call a radiant personality."

The woman agreed. She said, "You're right. How do you account for that?"

As they walked along further, the man stopped and pointed across the river. "Do you see that wonderful old castle? Well, when I was a young boy, my friends and I would love to sit on the riverbank and look at it in the evening. We were able to tell, in a way, what was going on by the number of lights that were burning. If just family members were home, only a few of the lights would be seen. If they were entertaining guests, there would be many lights, and the place would become magically beautiful."

The young man continued, "One time, the owners of the castle entertained royalty. You should have seen the lights! I have never seen such brilliance!"

As they continued their walk, the woman said, "I think the only way I could explain her radiant personality is that in the interior of her being, she is always entertaining a Royal Guest." The young man agreed.

Each of us, as Christians, is asked to reflect Jesus Christ. Each of us is to a "light to the world." As members of the "priesthood of all believers" via our baptism, we are to be "Other Christs."

The question is, though, how do we do this? How do we go about in the world reflecting Christ to others? How do we show that we are true followers of Jesus?

I believe there are three ways we can reflect Christ to others.

Realizing that darkness is the opposite of light, we get rid of the darkness. This means we strive to eliminate the negative characteristics of our lives. Some of the most common negative characteristics we face are impatience, materialism, greed, lacking concern for those in need, judging others, wasting time, failing to make the most of our lives, gossiping, and the like.

Second, we strive to replace the vices with virtues. To reflect Christ means we should strive to cultivate and nurture patience, charity, joy, forgiveness, mercy, kindness, gentleness, courage, fidelity, humility, and the like. This is a lifelong process, something we need to do every day. We will never arrive at perfection as human beings, but we are to continually strive to radiate Christian virtues as best we can.

And finally, we need to cultivate our Catholic faith. We do this by spiritual reading, retreats, Bible study, faith sharing groups, and others. There are many older American Catholics who stopped learning about their faith in grade school. Times change, and so do Catholic theologies. What was taught in 1915 is vastly different, in many areas of our faith, than in 2015. We need to keep up. We need to learn how to approach the complex problems of the modern world, problems that did not exist in ages past.

As we continue our lives this week, it would be a good idea to reflect on our own lives. How do we seek to be the lights of Christ to the world?

And that is the good news I have for you on this Twelfth Sunday in Ordinary Time.

Story source: Anonymous, "Entertaining Royalty," from *Light Sermon Illustrations* – MoreIllustrations.Com. April 2015.

Chapter 36

13th Sunday in Ordinary Time - A
St. Marguerite Bourgeoys

Scripture:

- 2 Kings 4: 8-11, 14-16a
- Psalm 89: 2-3, 16-17, 18-19
- Romans 6: 3-4, 8-11
- Matthew 10: 37-42

Today, Catholic Christians celebrate the Thirteenth Sunday in Ordinary Time.

In today's Gospel from Matthew, Jesus speaks to his disciples about the challenges of following him. After telling them that they must love him more than their family members, he assures them that they will receive a reward. Specifically, he says, "And whoever gives only a cup of cold water to one of these little ones to drink because the little one is a disciple—amen, I say to you, he will surely not lose his reward" (Matthew 10:42).

Today, we look at the inspirational life of a remarkable woman who heard the missionary call of Jesus. Her name was Marguerite Bourgeoys.

Marguerite was born in born in Troyes, France in 1620. After her mother died, she helped run the household and to care for her younger siblings. When she was twenty years old, she had a profound religious experience during a religious procession.

Marguerite tried to join the Poor Clares order, but they rejected her application. She also tried to become a Carmelite nun, but they too rejected her. Fortunately for Marguerite, though, she had a priest advisor who told her that her rejection to cloistered orders was perhaps a sign that God wanted her to lead an apostolic life, a missionary life, a life dedicated to serving God in a "hands-on" manner.

Following this advice, Marguerite began devoting herself to a local group of women who did charitable work for poor children and the sick in her town. These women were externs of a convent of cloistered nuns. Marguerite learned, from this experience, there were many apostolic works that people could not do if they were cloistered, and that it was not necessary to join an order to join in its religious and charitable works.

In 1653, the founder of Montreal, Canada passed through the town of Troyes and invited Marguerite to join him in Ville Marie, which is what Montreal was called then. There, she would be a lay teacher instructing the children of colonists and Native Americans Indians. So, in 1653, she began the 3-month journey to Canada.

In Canada, Marguerite's first school was in a stone stable that leaders of the town gave her for that purpose. Not only did she teach such basics as reading and writing, she also taught the children religion, values, and practical skills such as home economics. She was also a champion of education for all children. She gave special attention to girls and the poor.

Marguerite, however, did not limit herself to teaching in formal schools. In addition, she helped with faith formation in her parish and helped families learn skills necessary to run homes in the wilderness. She also served as the official guardian of orphan girls that the government sent her. Under her guidance, the girls learned the skills they would need to become successful homemakers. Because of all of her work in the New World, people began calling her "the Mother of the Colony."

Marguerite knew, however, that she could not do all of the work that needed to be done alone. She needed help. Therefore, she made some trips back to France to recruit other women to help her do missionary work in Canada.

Eventually, this group of women became formalized as a religious congregation – the Congregation of Notre Dame. Though the local bishop tried to get Marguerite to attach her congregation to a cloistered community, she refused. She knew that cloistered groups could not do the apostolic work of the Church. Because she stood her ground, her Order flourished, and the Church grew. Today, Quebec is one of the most Catholic places in the world.

In 1698, the Catholic Church approved the Congregation of Notre Dame, and the Sisters made their vows as non-cloistered religious. This Congregation has the honor of being the Church's first non-cloistered foreign missionary community for women. Today, the Order serves in many nations of Asia, the Americas, and Africa.

Marguerite died in Montreal in 1700. Pope Pius XII beatified Marguerite Bourgeoys in 1950, and Pope John Paul II canonized her on October 31, 1982 as the first Canadian woman saint. She is a patron saint of people rejected by religious orders, of people who are poor and those who fight against poverty, and of people who have lost parents. Her feast day is January 12.

The life of St. Marguerite Bourgeoys is a beautiful example of someone following Jesus as a missionary. Like so many lives of missionaries, it is also a testament to the triumph of the human spirit over incredible adversities.

But the life of St. Marguerite also shows us something often neglected in saintly literature: the way that God often closes a door so that one can walk through another that is so much better.

In Marguerite's life, two cloistered communities rejected her. Fortunately, a priest encouraged her to take this as a sign that she should live an apostolic, rather than cloistered, life. This shows how critical it is for priests to be sensitive to the vocational journeys of people. It also shows how one should never be crushed and defeated by rejection.

As we continue our life journeys this week, it would be a good idea to reflect on our journeys. How has God closed doors in our lives only to show us that another door holds so much more for us?

And that is the good news I have for you on this Thirteenth Sunday in Ordinary Time.

Story sources:

- "St. Marguerite Bourgeoys" in Catholic.Culture.org
- Matz, Terry, "St. Marguerite Bourgeoys," Saints & Angels, Catholic Online.

Chapter 37

14th Sunday in Ordinary Time - A
The Yoke and the Venard

Scripture:

- Zechariah 9: 9-10
- Psalm 145: 1-2, 8-9, 10-11, 13cd-14
- Romans 8: 9, 11-13
- Matthew 11: 25-30

Today Catholic Christians celebrate the Fourteenth Sunday in Ordinary Time.

On this Sunday, we hear Jesus telling his followers: "Come to me, all you who labor and are burdened, and I will give you rest. Take my yoke upon you and learn from me, for I am meek and humble of heart; and you will find rest for yourselves. For my yoke is easy, and my burden light" (Matthew 11: 28-30).

As a person who never lived in a rural area, I never actually experienced the concept of "yoke" until my recent mission trip to my parish's "sister parish" in Honduras. There, in a town called La Libertad, I watched two men put a yoke on two oxen. A yoke is a bar of wood constructed to unite two animals. This enables them to work together in the fields or on roads. These oxen pulled a cart used for carrying items.

Frequently throughout history, the word "yoke" has been used symbolically to refer to people being enslaved or mistreated. But Jesus says that his yoke is easy and his burden light. How can this be?

Jesus was saying that following him was not difficult. He was not insisting on all kinds of petty laws and rules and customs such as those the Scribes and Pharisees enforced. At the time of Jesus, the Jews had hundreds of religious laws of every kind. There were people who did nothing but ponder all of these laws and rules and customs to determine whether someone was a sinner or not.

Jesus, on the other hand, rejected this kind of mentality. He rejected slavery to laws and rituals and customs. Instead of being slaves to what he sometimes called "the letter of the law," he advocated a devotion to "the spirit of the law." This emphasis has led Catholic Christians to reject the kind of fundamentalist thinking that leads people to worship laws and customs and rituals and, at times, even churches or religious figures.

But how can we talk about having on a yoke but the burden being light? Well, there was one time in my own life that I was freer than I have ever been, and that was during my high school years.

When I was fourteen years old, I left home and went to a Maryknoll Junior Seminary in the mountains of Pennsylvania. It was nicknamed "The Venard" after a nineteenth-century French missionary-martyr, Theophane Venard. There I lived an incredibly regimented life. We had classes six days a week, though we had time off on Wednesday and

Saturday afternoons. There were times and places we had to be silent, and we could not talk during meals unless we had permission.

The faculty opened letters we received before we received them, and our outgoing mail was also checked.

Bells were called "the voice of God," commanding us when to get up in the morning and when to go to bed at night, when to go to class, when to study and when to work, when to go to chapel and when to go to the refectory to eat. The bells regulated every day.

Our study hall times were also highly regimented. Each of us, for example, had a record of what we were to study on which days and which hours. If it were Thursday at 7:30 p.m., for example, I might be scheduled to study Pennsylvania history, while at 8:15 p.m. I might be scheduled to study French.

Now you might be wondering how in the world I could consider such a period of my life as the freest time of my life. For many people, this pre-Vatican II seminary life seems more like prison than anything else.

So why was it so incredibly joyful and free for me?

First, I was at peace knowing that I was following God's plan for me. Nothing can give one a greater sense of serenity or peace than following what one believes is God's plan for them. Although it was not God's will for me to become a Maryknoll priest, it was his will that I should have a robust foundation to begin several years of formation in the world that would one day lead me to a very special type of priesthood, a priesthood that will continue to unfold in fascinating and important ways through the years.

Second, this environment was perfect for a creative person. Because we did not have to make basic decisions about daily life—what to eat, when to get up, what to study, what to wear, when to do various things—our minds could be free to explore the world of books, ideas and friendships.

And third, when one is free from the ordinary concerns of daily life, one is free to explore God in exciting and intimate ways. Walking in the woods or beside a lake, one can pray the rosary in silence or with friends. One can meditate in chapel and talk with the Lord and then listen to his response. One can read all kinds of spiritual works and biographies of saints and other heroes. In summary, the regimentation of ordinary things led to freedom in extraordinary things, producing one of the freest times of my life.

As we continue our life journeys this week, it would be a good idea to take some time to reflect on our own life. How free are we? Do we find following the Lord a burden or a joy?

That is the good news I have for you on this Fourteenth Sunday in Ordinary Time.

Chapter 38

15th Sunday in Ordinary Time - A
St. Giuseppe Moscati

Scripture:

- Isaiah 55: 10-11
- Psalm 65: 10abcd, 10e-11, 12-13, 14
- Romans 8: 18-23
- Matthew 13: 1-23

Today as Catholic Christians celebrate the Fifteenth Sunday in Ordinary Time, we encounter rich imagery from the Book of Isaiah and the Gospel of Matthew.

Now in Biblical times, people had a very specific cosmology, or idea of how the universe was made. Specifically, they thought there were three realms: Heaven was where God or the gods lived; Earth was where humans lived; and the Underworld was where the dead lived. They believed the world was flat and there were pillars holding up a canopy called the sky. They believed the sun traveled across the canopy to the underworld and then came back to its resting point. Surrounding the Earth were chaotic waters.

Although this view of creation was incorrect from a scientific point of view, that is okay, for the Bible is not a science book. Rather, it is a theology book, a book that seeks to explain God and God's will for us. And in today's selection from Isaiah, we hear that rain and snow come down from heaven to make a change in the Earth, to make it fertile and fruitful. As a result of the rain interacting with the seeds of the Earth, grain can grow and, from that, we can have bread to eat. Likewise, God's word comes down from heaven to Earth so that human beings will know God's will for them and act accordingly. In other words, though the people in Biblical times did not have the scientific knowledge we have today, they did understand the concept of cause-and-effect.

Likewise, in the Gospel passage, Jesus uses the imagery of seeds being sown on different types of ground. The seeds that fall on good ground produce much fruit. Needless to say, the moral of the parable is that we should be like the good soil and be fruitful members of the kingdom of God here on Earth.

Throughout the two thousand year history of Catholic Christianity, we have always had many people who have listened to God's word, incorporated it into their lives, and been fruitful in great measure. Though we often hear about priests and nuns and martyrs as saints, we don't often hear about laypersons who live the single life in extraordinary ways. One such man was Giuseppe Moscati.

Giuseppe was born the seventh of nine children in 1880. His father was a lawyer and a judge, and his mother was of noble birth. When he was four years old, the family moved to Naples, where Giuseppe spent most of his life.

In 1892, Giuseppe's brother, Alberto, fell from a horse while in the military and suffered an incurable head trauma. After helping care for his brother for some time, Giuseppe decided to become a physician. He received his doctorate in medicine from the University of Naples in 1903.

After he became a physician, Giuseppe began working at a hospital for incurable cases, and eventually he became an administrator of the hospital. When he was not seeing patients, he conducted medical research. He always attended daily Mass and Communion, a practice he developed as a child.

In 1906, when Mount Vesuvius erupted, Giuseppe rushed to a hospital near the volcano to evacuate the elderly and paralytic patients. The patients all got out just before the roof collapsed. He became even more famous in 1911 when a cholera epidemic broke out in Naples. The government asked him to perform public health inspections to see what was causing the epidemic. He immediately went to work investigating the origins of the disease and how to cure it. He was very happy when the government put his findings into practice. In the same year, 1911, Giuseppe received a second doctoral degree, this time in the field of physiological chemistry.

In 1912 or 1913, Giuseppe decided to make a vow of celibacy, promising never to marry. For a while, he thought of become a Jesuit, but the Jesuits told him he could do more for humanity as a physician. In 1914, when his mother died from diabetes, Giuseppe began to experiment with insulin in the treatment of the disease.

During World War I, Giuseppe cared for or visited over 3,000 wounded soldiers.

Giuseppe had a strong belief that the soul of a person was much more important than the body. He said, "One must attend first to the salvation of the soul and only then to that of the body." He practiced what he preached, and he became known as "the holy doctor of Naples." He had a special love for the poor and the homeless, and he absolutely refused to charge any fee for the poor or for priests or Religious. In fact, he would often slip a little money inside the envelope he gave to poor patients along with their prescriptions.

On April 12, 1927, Giuseppe attended his usual morning Mass, received Communion, and spent the morning at the hospital. He saw patients in the afternoon and then sat down to rest. He never woke up.

Giuseppe was canonized in 1987 following the miraculous cure of an ironworker dying of leukemia. The young man's mother had a dream of a doctor in a white coat curing her son. She identified the doctor as Giuseppe Moscati after seeing a photograph of him. Her son was cured and able to return to work.

Today, many people believe that Giuseppe is still conducting office hours from his new office in heaven.

As we continue our life journeys this week, it would be good to reflect how the word of God is touching our hearts and leading us to live our vocations as well as Giuseppe lived his.

And that is the good news I have for you on this Fifteenth Sunday in Ordinary Time.

Story sources:

- Miller, Michael. "Joseph Moscati: Saint, Doctor, and Miracle-Worker." *Lay Witness Magazine*. Reprinted in Catholic Education Resource Center, 2004.
- Ray, Paul A. & Bottesi, Andre J. "St. Giuseppe Moscati, The Holy Physician of Naples." Catholic.net, 2013.

Chapter 39

16th Sunday in Ordinary Time - A
Fifty-Seven Cent Church

Scripture:

- Wisdom 12: 13, 16-19
- Psalm 86: 5-6, 9-10, 15-16
- Romans 8: 26-27
- Matthew 13: 24-43

Today as we gather to celebrate the Eucharist on this Sixteenth Sunday in Ordinary Time, we encounter three fascinating parables of Jesus in the Gospel of Matthew. In these parables, Jesus is trying to give the crowds a glimpse into the nature of the kingdom of heaven.

In each of the parables, the main theme is that of growth. The kingdom of heaven, which begins in this lifetime on Earth, is not something stagnant. Rather, it must grow because it is alive. Thus, the little mustard seed does not simply exist in its present state. Rather, it grows into a bush big enough for birds to nest in. Likewise, yeast produces change in the wheat flour so that it can become bread. And in the parable of the weeds growing with the wheat, the wheat will triumph in spite of the weeds.

From these three parables, we learn that what we do must produce not just growth, but healthy growth. We are supposed to grow in virtue, and we are to build up Christ's Church. One little girl showed how this was done. Her name was Hattie May Wiatt.

Hattie Mae Wiatt lived in the nineteenth century in Philadelphia. One day, she tried to go to Sunday school at a church near her home. Unfortunately, the little girl could not get in because there was no room.

As she stood there crying in her shabby clothes, the pastor of the church, Russell H. Cromwell, happened to walk by. When he found out what she wanted, he picked her up and carried her into the church and made room for her in the class. Hattie Mae was incredibly happy that the pastor had found room for her, and that night before she fell asleep, she could not help but think of all the children who could not learn about Jesus because there was no room at the little church for them.

Two years later, little Hattie Mae Wiatt died in her poor tenement building. When Hattie Mae's body was being moved, the people made a startling discovery. They found an old red purse that Hattie Mae must have found in a trashcan. Inside was a note and fifty-seven cents that Hattie Mae must have been saving over a two-year period. The note, scribbled in her little-girl handwriting, said, "This is to help build the little church bigger so more children can go to Sunday school."

Needless to say, the pastor was quite touched by this precious little love offering of Hattie Mae. What sacrifices she must have made to save this meager fifty-seven cents, and what joy she must have felt each time she had an extra penny to put into the worn-out red purse.

The pastor took the note and the purse to church and challenged the deacons to begin to raise money for a new church.

Soon a newspaper learned about the story and a wealthy realtor gave land worth many thousands of dollars. Soon church members, along with others who had read the newspaper story, began making donations. Soon the church had raised a quarter of a million dollars—a huge fortune in those days.

The fifty-seven cents that a little girl with the dream had saved had grown to be enough for a new church that would allow many more children to attend Sunday school classes. In fact, not only was the church able to build a huge church that could seat 3,300 people, it also was able to build a university to educate others. This institution of higher education is known as Temple University. And the good news did not stop there. With additional money, Good Samaritan Hospital was formed to provide health care for the people of Philadelphia, along with a Sunday school building where Hattie Mae's picture rests.

Now you and I probably will not be called by God to build a university, and fortunately we already have the most beautiful church in our diocese. However, like little Hattie Mae, God too has given us a challenge. Our current challenge is to make it possible for the two priests of our sister parish in Honduras to be able to travel to the 87churches and chaples in the parish, to celebrate Mass and other sacraments. The priests, who have never asked for a single thing from our parish and have always been incredibly grateful for every penny and prayer we can offer, have come to us to beg for help. What they need is a new pickup truck. They have one, but it is not sufficient because there are two priests to cover the 87 churches in the mountains.

Therefore, we are challenged to come up with the $24,000 it will take to make this dream a reality. I ask you all to consider making a donation to helping our two sister parish priests bring Christ to their people. We are their only hope. They each earn only $50 per month. The cost of a new truck strong enough for the treacherous mountain roads is completely out of their reach unless we can help them. If you would like to help fund this project, please contact the parish office or me.

The good news is, of course, that we will be able to help them. How soon we can do so is the only question.

That is the good news I have for you on this Sixteenth Sunday in Ordinary Time.

Story source: Russell H. Conwell, "The History of Fifty-seven Cents Sunday morning sermon at Grace Baptist Church, Philadelphia, December 1, 1912. Internet source.

Chapter 40

17th Sunday in Ordinary Time - A
Solomon and Wisdom

Scripture:

- 1 Kings 3: 5, 7-12
- Psalm 119: 57 & 72, 76-77, 127-128, 129-130
- Romans 8: 28-30
- Matthew 13: 44-52

Today as Catholic Christians gather to celebrate the Eucharist on this Seventeenth Sunday in Ordinary Time, we encounter one of the most fascinating figures in the Bible, King Solomon. In the Old Testament reading for today, we read that the wisdom of Solomon was so great, that God proclaimed that he was not only the wisest person of his time, he was wiser than every human being before him and every human being who would ever come after him. That is indeed an amazing statement from God! Therefore, it would be good to learn more about Solomon before examining the virtue of wisdom.

Solomon lived almost one thousand years before Jesus. He was the son of King David and Bathsheba. When he grew up, he became a King even though he was not the eldest of David's sons.

Some of Solomon's great achievements were building the temple in Jerusalem and writing three books of the Bible: the *Song of Songs, Proverbs,* and *Ecclesiastes.* Solomon was also known as one of the richest men of his time.

But Solomon, whom God saw as the wisest man who ever lived, also had a thousand wives—seven hundred regular wives and three hundred minor wives, called "concubines"! Now when we look around our country today, we see that even one spouse is one too many for millions of people, so the concept of one thousand spouses absolutely boggles the mind. And when one remembers that this was the man whom God proclaimed the wisest man of the whole human race forever, we can only say, "The mind of God is truly not the same as the mind of man."

But that is not what this homily is about. It's about "wisdom." Solomon, though famous for many things, is most famous for his wisdom. We all know the story of the two women who were fighting over custody of a baby, for both claimed to be the baby's mother. Solomon, in his wisdom, said the solution was to cut the baby in half, and then each woman would be able to have half a baby. One woman was very pleased with this solution, while the other was horrified and asked that instead of cutting the baby in two, the other woman should have the baby. Solomon figured that the real mother would never have her child killed, so he gave the baby to the mother who would rather give the baby away alive than have it killed.

Now since God obviously values the virtue of wisdom, and because we should strive to be wise people, it would be good to define it and explore a few characteristics of wisdom.

Wisdom may be defined as the quality of judging rightly and following the soundest course of action. Possessing knowledge does not guarantee wisdom, nor does being "smart" and quick to catch on. Many of us know highly educated people who are very unwise, as they do not follow a good course of action in their lives. On the other hand, many of us know deeply wise people who do not even know how to read and write, yet live their lives in abundance of joy. Here are things to think about when examining wisdom.

First, because wisdom often comes from making mistakes, often repeatedly, it is usually something we see in older adults much more frequently than we see it in children or youth. However, there are many examples of children and youth exhibiting wisdom from a very early age.

In one family I know, for example, there were two sisters who grew up in the same household. One of them was very frugal with her money, and she always had enough money to buy the things she liked. The other one, however, let money slip through her fingers like water. She was continually broke and always in need of an advance on her allowance. How one sibling is wise in terms of money while another is not is a mystery to me.

Second, wise people usually have a deep understanding of human nature and develop a plan based on this understanding. For example, every November and December people write to advice columnists about dreading upcoming trips to relatives' houses for the holidays. They talk about how certain family members always "push their buttons" by making snide comments, criticizing them or their families, getting drunk, making unwanted advances on them, or whatever. Yet despite having a miserable time at these family gatherings every year, the unwise letter-writers continue to put themselves and their families into these toxic situations. The wise person, however, realizes that the people who make them miserable will be the same this year as they have been in years past. Therefore, wise persons come up with a mature plan—such as declining to participate in other households' holiday traditions—and stay at home and develop holiday traditions unique to their own immediate families.

And third, wise people are noted for being known more for their listening than their speaking. They know that is perfectly fine to say, "I don't know" when they don't know something. They know topics to steer clear of at family gatherings, such as politics or sex or religion, if they know these are touchy topics. They know they can learn more from listening than from speaking.

As we continue our life journeys this week, it would be a good idea to think of the wisest persons we know. What qualities do they possess that leads us to say they are wise?

And that is the good news I have for you on this Seventeenth Sunday in Ordinary Time.

Chapter 41

18th Sunday in Ordinary Time - A
The Weather Vane

Scripture:

- Isaiah 55: 1-3
- Psalm 145: 8-9, 15-16, 17-18
- Romans 8: 35, 37-39
- Matthew 14: 13-21

As Catholic Christians come together today to celebrate the Eucharist on this Eighteenth Sunday in Ordinary Time, we read a beautiful passage from the Book of Isaiah. In this passage, we hear the Lord telling us that everybody is invited to come to him. It doesn't matter if you don't have money; you'll be fed plenty. If we come to the Lord, Isaiah continues:

> "Come to me heedfully,
> listen, that you may have life.
> I will renew with you
> the everlasting covenant,
> the benefits assured to David" (Isaiah 55: 3).

In the Gospel passage today, we hear how Jesus went about making this passage from Isaiah come true. First, the Scripture shows how Jesus had a great following. When he tried to get away for some quiet time, the crowds followed him. Like moths to the light, the people were attracted to Jesus. Later, when he wanted to feed thousands of people, he took two fish and five loaves of bread and fed them with plenty left over.

The message of both of these Scripture passages is that with God, we have what we need. God's bounty will never run out. Unfortunately, though, we sometimes forget that God's love and bounty will never leave us. God is watching over us always. But when we forget this important principle, we become troubled. We are not at peace. We lack joy and gratitude. This is something that a pastor needed to be reminded of in the following story.

One beautiful sunny autumn day, a pastor went for a walk in the countryside with a long-time friend. As they walked through the rolling hills of the farmland, the pastor noticed a barn with a weather vane on its roof. At the top of the weather vane were the words, "God is love."

The pastor remarked to his friend that he thought this was not an appropriate place for such a message. He said, "Weather vanes change with the wind, but God's love is constant."

The pastor's friend walked along in silence for a little bit before he replied, "I don't agree with you about those words. I think you misunderstand the meaning. The weather vane is simply indicating a truth: no matter which way the wind blows, God is love, and such love is constant."

The pastor's friend had a good deal of wisdom, for indeed, God's love is everywhere, and we should always place this first in our lives.

As a sociologist, a psychiatric-mental health nurse, a writer, and a priest, I have always been incredibly fascinated by the study of human beings. Of all God's creatures, humans are by far the most interesting to me. People who are true reflections of Christ fascinate me. Here are just three characteristics that such people tend to share.

First, they are not attached to the things of this world. Though they own material things, they never let material things own them. They tend to live *below* their means—which is, by the way, the new financial model advocated by American financial gurus today. Such people can be just as happy with a bologna sandwich as they can be with a five-course steak dinner with all the trimmings. Needless to say, they are the kind of people who do not find themselves in debt from credit and debit cards.

Second, they are joyful people. To be joyful, one must be "comfortable in one's skin." They know who they are, and they are grateful to God for who they are. They don't have to make people think they are more than they are. If they can't afford the same things that their friends or coworkers or neighbors can afford, they don't feel bad. They don't wear masks, pretending to be something they are not. Such people are delighted to be part of the universe, and they show this joy through their gratitude and generosity to those in need. They are the givers of the universe rather than the takers.

And third, they radiate joy to others. Whenever I encounter such Christ-like people, I am happy about the encounter. I never feel bad after an encounter with them. Such people have a good sense of humor. They are sensitive and compassionate. They talk about ideas instead of gossip. They never present themselves as "holier-than-thou" or superior to others. They are down-to-earth, as comfortable as an old shoe. After an encounter with such people, I can't help but examine my own life and how I'm living it, and I can't help but strive to "catch" some of their serenity, peace and joy.

As we continue our life journeys this week, it would be a good idea to take some time alone and ask ourselves who in our lives radiates the peace and joy of Christ. What are the things that lead us to put them in the "Christ-like" category? How can we be more Christ-like in our own lives?

And that is the good news I have for you on this Eighteenth Sunday in Ordinary Time.

Story source: Anonymous, "God is Love," in Brian Cavanaugh's *Sower's Seeds of Encouragement: Fifth Planting,* 1998, #34, p. 31.

Chapter 42

19th Sunday in Ordinary Time - A
Jesus and the Storms of Life

Scripture:

- 1 Kings 19: 9a, 11-13a
- Psalm 85: 9ab-10, 11-12, 13-14
- Romans 9: 1-5
- Matthew 14: 22-33

Today as Catholic Christians come to celebrate the Eucharist on the Nineteenth Sunday in Ordinary Time, we encounter the fascinating story of Peter and Jesus walking on the water.

The scene is a stormy sea, and the time is "the fourth watch" of the night. The "fourth watch" refers to the period of time between 3 a.m. and 6 a.m. In other words, it was dark outside as the storm raged. Peter and his colleagues were far from shore, being tossed about in their boat. Suddenly, the disciples saw Jesus walking on the water to them, and they cried out in fear. At first they thought they must be seeing a ghost, but Jesus called out for them not to be afraid. Peter then said, "Lord, if it is you, command me to come to you on the water" (Matthew 14: 28). Jesus did as Peter asked, and Peter got out of the boat and began walking on the water to Jesus. He was doing just fine until he became distracted by the winds blowing all around him. Then his faith left him, and he began to sink. Jesus, however, saved him.

This story always reminds me of cartoon characters who are being chased by someone. They run right off a cliff, but continue running through the air until they realize they are in the air. When this happens, they suddenly remember that they are not supposed to be able to do what they are actually doing. Then, they fall to the ground.

Peter's story is filled with rich symbolism of faith: the storms of life we all experience; the darkness that comes just before the light; and God's love and care for us. Sometimes we need to look at our lives and remember our faith. That is what the boy in the following story by Mark Hansen reminded his father.

In 1988 there was a terrible earthquake in Armenia that killed over 30,000 people in less than four minutes.

One young father, when he heard about the earthquake, rushed to his son's school. When he got there, he found the school building flat as a pancake. After his initial shock, he remembered a promise that he had made to his son, "No matter what, I'll always be there for you!"

The young father rushed to the part of the building where his son's classroom had been, and began digging through the rubble.

As he began digging, other parents showed up clutching their hearts and crying out things like, "My son!" or "My daughter!" Many well-meaning parents tried to pull him away saying such things as, "It's too late!" or "They're dead!" or "You can't help!" or "Go home!" or "Face reality, there's nothing you can do!" or "You'll only make things worse!"

The young father did not pay attention to all the well-meaning parents. He just kept digging and asking each and every person, "Will you please help me?"

The fire chief tried to get him to go home, as he was afraid the building would blow up. The father simply said, "Will you help me?" The police chief also tried to get the father to stop removing the stones from the rubble, but the young father refused to give up. He dug for eight hours... twelve hours...twenty-four hours...thirty-six hours. On the thirty-eighth hour, he heard his son's voice. He screamed his son's name, "Armand!" A boy's voice called back, "Dad? It's me, Dad! I told the other kids not to worry. I told them that if you were alive, you'd save me, and when you saved me, they'd be saved too. You promised, 'No matter what, I'll always be there for you!' You did it, Dad!"

The dad learned that fourteen out of the thirty-three in Armand's class were still alive. When the building collapsed, it made a wedge, like a triangle, and that saved the children.

The young father called to his son, "Come on out, son!"

The son, Armand, replied, "No, Dad! Let the other kids out first because I know you'll get me. No matter what, I know you'll be there for me!"

This beautiful story, along with the story of Jesus and Peter walking on the water, reminds us of many things. Here are just three.

First, in this world we will always encounter storms. Our faith will not prevent them. Our faith will, however, help us cope with them.

Second, the darkness that accompanies the storms of life will eventually give way to light. If you have ever suffered depression, you may have likened your experience to being in a dark tunnel that seems to have no light at the end. Eventually, though, you discovered that indeed there was light at the end. After you have experienced this many times, you will remember that in the darkest days, there will be better ones.

And third, we are reminded that though suffering is part of life on this planet, God is always with us. Though we may not be able to see God because of the pitch-black night, God is always able to see us.

As we continue our life journey this week, it would be a good idea to reflect on the storms of our lives—past and present. How have these experiences made us spiritually stronger? How has God shown his presence to us?

And that is the good news I have for you on this Nineteenth Sunday in Ordinary Time.

Story source: Mark Hansen, "Are You Going To Help Me?" in *Chicken Soup for the Soul*, 1993, pp. 273-274.

Chapter 43

20th Sunday in Ordinary Time - A
Harry the Usher

Scripture:

- Isaiah 56: 1, 6-7
- Psalm 67: 2-3, 5, 6 & 8
- Romans 11: 13-15, 29-32
- Matthew 15: 21-28

Today as Catholic Christians come to celebrate the Eucharist on this Twentieth Sunday in Ordinary Time, we encounter three Scripture selections that have the same theme of welcome.

"Catholic" means "universal." The early Christian churches began to call all of the churches "The Catholic Church" as early as 100 A.D. To be called "universal" is a call to be <u>inclusive</u> rather than <u>exclusive</u>. In other words, all are welcome to be part of the Body of Christ on Earth.

Sometimes, however, we forget to be welcoming to others. Therefore, it is good every once in awhile to hear a story that reminds us how important it is to welcome others in our midst. That is what we see in the story of "Harry the Usher" as told by Fr. William J. Bausch.

There was once a pastor who received a letter that was marked, "Please give to Harry the Usher." When Harry opened the letter that the pastor had given him, he read the following:

> *Dear Harry,*
>
> *I'm sorry I don't know your last name, but then, you don't know mine. I'm Gert, Gert at the ten o'clock Mass every Sunday. I'm writing to ask a favor. I don't know the priests too well, but somehow feel close to you. I don't know how you got to know my first name, but every Sunday morning you smile and greet me by name, and we exchange a few words: how bad the weather is, how much you like my hat, and how I am late on a particular Sunday. I just wanted to say thank you for taking the time to remember an old woman, for the smiles, for your consideration, for your thoughtfulness.*
>
> *Now for the favor. I am dying, Harry. My husband has been dead for sixteen years, and the kids are scattered. It is very important to me that when they bring me to church for the last time, you will be there to say, "Hello, Gert. Good to see you." If you are there, Harry, I will feel assured that your warm hospitality will be duplicated in my new home in heaven. With love and gratitude, Gert.*

What a beautiful story this is, for it teaches us many things.

First, there is no such thing as an "unimportant" ministry in the Church. Each one of us has various gifts or talents, and there are no gifts that we are to hoard only for ourselves. When we share these gifts for building up the Kingdom of God on Earth, we are said to be doing ministry. And every person who is baptized is an official, anointed minister of the Church. Whether we are making baptismal stoles behind the scenes or standing in front of an assembly as a lector, our ministry is important. Oftentimes we do different ministries at different times in our lives, and most of us do multiple ministries.

Second, it's good to remember that for many people, coming to church on the weekend is the only first-hand experience they have with parish life. Therefore, what they encounter when they come to worship is how they perceive a parish. Every week we have a wonderful number of visitors. How they are treated will define how they perceive the parish. Many times people tell me about how Parish X is "unfriendly" or how Parish Y is "friendly." How they arrived at these classifications was in great part due to how people around them acted towards them when they visited at Sunday Mass.

In North Carolina, only five percent of Catholic Christians were born in North Carolina: almost all of us come from somewhere else. And because the Diocese of Raleigh is one of the fastest-growing dioceses in the United States, people are continually entering our area searching for a parish in which they feel comfortable, in which they can grow and flourish. Maybe you will be the one who "makes or breaks" their good experience when it's time for the Sign of Peace. Greeting people around you with a smile and a handshake is an incredibly important ministry.

And third, because humans tend to be exclusionary in their behavior, we must always fight against that tendency. All of us compose the Catholic Church, the Universal Church. That means that we are open to all people. It is true that in the past many Catholic parishes did not live up to their Catholic name. For example, we know full well that there were racially segregated Catholic parishes.

Thankfully we have moved beyond race-segregated congregations, but there will always be people within our midst who are not genuinely Catholic in their outlook. They are the ones who would like to exclude people because of their language, country of origin, political perspectives, sexual orientation, marital status, age, handicaps, or whatever. As Catholic Christians, we will not tolerate such discrimination in our parish.

As we continue our life journeys this week, it would be good to ask ourselves how we practice the virtue of welcoming in our lives.

And that is the good news I have for you on this Twentieth Sunday in Ordinary Time.

Story source: "Harry the Usher," in William J. Bausch's *A World of Stories for Preachers and Teachers*, 1998, #221, pp. 334-335.

Chapter 44

21st Sunday in Ordinary Time - A
St. John XXIII

Scripture:

- Isaiah 22: 19-23
- Psalm 138: 1-2a, 2bc & 3, 6 & 8bc
- Romans 11: 33-36
- Matthew 16: 13-20

As Catholic Christians come to celebrate the Eucharist on this Twenty-First Sunday in Ordinary Time, we hear Jesus make a remarkable statement to the Apostle Peter: "And so I say to you, you are Peter, and upon this rock I will build my church, and the gates of the netherworld shall not prevail against it. I will give you the keys to the kingdom of heaven. Whatever you bind on earth shall be bound in heaven, and whatever you loose on earth shall be loosed in heaven" (Matthew 16: 18-19).

For Catholic Christians, this passage indicates the founding of the papacy with Peter being the first "papa" of the Christian communities, which, by around 100 A.D., were called The Catholic Church.

Through the centuries, the papacy has undergone many changes. There have been many holy popes, and there have been many scoundrels. Some popes have had peaceful reigns, while others have had tremendous opposition that led to their banishment or even to martyrdom. There have been popes who have been very rigorist or legalistic in their approach to church life, while there have been many who were very pastoral.

One pope who was a great model of a loving, pastoral leader was a man of our own time, John XXIII.

Angelo Giuseppe Roncalli was born in 1881 in a small country village in the Lombardi region of Italy. Angelo's family worked as poor sharecroppers.

In 1904, Angelo was ordained a priest and worked as a secretary to the Bishop of Bergamo. He also was a lecturer at the diocesan seminary in that city and publisher of the diocesan newspaper.

In World War I, Fr. Angelo was drafted into the Royal Italian Army as a sergeant and served as both a chaplain and as a stretcher-bearer. After he was discharged from the army, he was named spiritual director of his seminary.

In 1921, Pope Benedict XV appointed him as the Italian President of the Society for the Propagation of the Faith. From that time on, Fr. Angelo was appointed to a succession of important Church positions and, in 1925, he became a bishop.

In 1935 he was made Apostolic Delegate to Turkey and Greece, and he used this position to help the Jewish underground save thousands of Jews from slaughter. In 1953, Pope Pius XII named him a Cardinal.

When Pope Pius XII died in 1958, cardinals from around the world gathered to elect a new pope. They decided to elect a "stop-gap" pope, one who would serve only a short while. The cardinals elected Angelo Giuseppe Roncalli, much to his amazement. Angelo, who would be the Church's 262nd pope, took the name John after his father and the parish church where he was baptized.

From the beginning, John XXIII was a popular pope noted for his pastoral sensitivity and devotion to the most vulnerable in society: children, the poor, the sick, and prisoners. Pope John was also noted for sneaking out of the Vatican late at night to walk around the streets of Rome. This gave him the nickname of "Johnny Walker," a pun on a popular liquor brand of the same name.

John XXIII was also noted for his wonderful sense of humor and down-to-earth style. For example, when a reporter asked him how many people worked at the Vatican, the pope replied, "Oh, no more than half of them." He also loved to take visitors down to the wine cellars of Vatican City for refreshments.

What John XXIII is most famous for, however, is calling the Second Vatican Council that ran from 1962 to 1965. This Council modernized the Church in many ways, but also called the Church to return to many ancient practices of the Catholic Church. For example, the Council asked Catholic Christians to go back to celebrating liturgy in the languages of the people, as the early Catholic Christians did. Most Catholic Christians readily followed John XXIII's lead and did, indeed, embrace the ancient Church practices.

John XXIII, who died on June 3, 1963 at the age of 81, did not live to the end of the Council. Pope John Paul II beatified John in 2000, and Pope Francis canonized him in 2014.

When we look at the life of a pope such as John XXIII, we find much to admire. First, we admire his pastoral sensitivity. Unlike many of his predecessors who were emotionally distant, John XXIII never forgot the "little guy," the members of society most in need of the help of the Church.

Second, Pope John XXIII showed the world that slavery to rules and regulations, and a harsh enforcement of such rules and regulations, was not the best way to create change. Rather, charity was a much better approach. This approach reminds us of the words of Jesus when he said that the Sabbath was made for humans, not humans made for the Sabbath. When confronted with controversies, John XXIII reiterated the words of St. Augustine: "In essentials unity, in doubtful things liberty, but in all things charity."

And third, though popes need to make important administrative decisions such as creating dioceses, working with governments of the world, and creating bishops and policies, they should foremost be good shepherds, putting the needs of "Everyone" ahead of their own.

As we continue our life journey this week, it would be a good time to reflect on how we ask God to guide the pope in making wise and loving decisions that respect the dignity and rights of all people, not just the majorities and powerful of the world.

And that is the good news I have for you on this Twenty-First Sunday in Ordinary Time.

Story sources:

- "St. John XXIII." Saints & Angels, Catholic Online.
- "St. John XXIII." Saint of the Day, AmericanCatholic.org.

Chapter 45

22nd Sunday in Ordinary Time - A
Crosses

Scripture:

- Jeremiah 20: 7-9
- Psalm 63: 2, 3-4, 5-6, 8-9
- Romans 12: 1-2
- Matthew 16: 21-27

Today as Catholic Christians come to celebrate the Eucharist on this Twenty-Second Sunday in Ordinary Time, we hear about the concept of suffering in all three readings from Sacred Scripture.

In the Old Testament, we hear about poor Jeremiah the prophet. He was most unhappy that he was treated so badly by those he tried to serve. In the epistle, Paul tells the people they should offer their bodies as living sacrifices. And in the Gospel, Jesus tells us that in order to follow him, we must take up our crosses.

Now suffering or crosses are something all of us have; no one is immune from them. Crosses of our lives can be anything from addictions to substances or behaviors to fears and worries. Some crosses are chronic, sufferings we carry around year after year, while others are transitory things that happen today and are gone tomorrow. Whether our crosses are chronic or transitory, severe or light, we are called to take them up. Taking them up means that we are to deal with them rather than to ignore them or let them destroy us.

Unfortunately, some people do not "take up" their crosses, and as a result, the crosses destroy them. That is what happened to the man in the following story from Fr. Brian Cavanaugh.

There was once a man we'll call George. George's wife died after they had been happily married for many years. During the two years following his wife's death, George was alert, intelligent, and physically healthy. He was also, however, desperately unhappy.

One day, George took a very bad fall. Although the physicians said that the injuries were not that serious, three days later George was dead. Many people who knew George said that he had simply quit living because he had abandoned any hope of ever being happy again. He did not die from the fall, but rather died from severe loneliness. He died because his life had become a series of days empty of happiness.

The saddest part of George's story was that in one way, he chose loneliness. After his wife died, family and friends gave him a lot of support. They encouraged him to get involved in groups and clubs, and they invited him out to dinner and on trips. But although George always found an excuse for not getting involved in life he would lament his loneliness in the next breath. His friends could only conclude that in large part, George had created his prison of isolation and loneliness.

From this story, as well as the Scripture passages of the day, we can make at least three suggestions about the concept of "crosses" or struggles in our lives.

First, we need to identify the crosses in our lives. After all, we can't very well take up our crosses if we don't know what they are. Maybe our cross is our worry about an adult child who has fallen away from the Church or who is suffering from a bad marriage. Or we may be in a bad marriage, living a life devoid of joy or hope. Or maybe we feel trapped in a job that we don't like. Perhaps we are being crushed under a mountain of debt that we racked up from reckless spending, a loss of job, medical problems, or college loans. Maybe our problem is an addiction to alcohol or other mind-altering drugs. Maybe we suffer from compulsive gossip or judging others in contrast to the commandments of Jesus Christ. Maybe our biggest problem is procrastination or greed or selfishness. The list of life's problems is endless. The point is, we cannot "take up" our crosses without first identifying them.

Second, we need to "take up" our crosses. "Taking up" one's crosses does not mean we are to simply accept them without examination. On the contrary, "taking up" one's crosses means that we are to look at them very carefully and determine which crosses we can change and which we cannot.

Most people will be amazed at how many of life's problems can be changed. For example, many worries and feelings of being overwhelmed by life's responsibilities come from procrastination. Procrastination, in turn, often comes from feelings of inadequacy for the task or fears of failure. When we get busy and get done what needs to get done, many of our crosses disappear. Likewise, sins such as gossip or judging others can be eliminated in our lives, thus saving us much grief.

There are also some crosses in our lives that we cannot change. Unfortunately, many people don't deal well with them because they have not come to the conclusion that they have no ability to influence these problems. They think they can change people, places, and things when actually they cannot. The frustration of not being able to change them may be more painful than the problems themselves. Knowing what one can't change, and turning those crosses over to God, can bring incredible peace.

And third, we should always try to focus on our blessings with a thankful heart. If we only focus on our crosses, we can become bitter, resentful, angry, and hostile.

As we continue our life journey this week, it would be a good idea to identify our crosses. How do we deal or not deal with them?

And that is the good news I have for you on this Twenty-Second Sunday in Ordinary Time.

Chapter 46

23rd Sunday in Ordinary Time - A
The Dying Ember

Scripture:

- Ezekiel 33: 7-9
- Psalm 95: 1-2, 6-7c, 7d-9
- Romans 13: 8-10
- Matthew 18: 15-20

Today as Catholic Christians come to celebrate the Eucharist, we hear a number of themes in the Scripture passages of today. In the Old Testament reading from the prophet Ezekiel, we hear about trying to help others who have lost their way, who are taking a life journey that is harmful. This theme is also present in the Gospel passage from St. Matthew. In the Gospel reading we also hear about the concept of forgiveness, prayer, and the real presence of Jesus in the community. Most importantly, though, we hear about the supremacy of love above all other virtues.

As Jesus said in many different ways, the entire Old Testament laws and prophecies can be summed up in the triple love commandment, that is, to love God, to love our neighbor, and to love ourselves. If we don't love, we don't follow Jesus.

Each of us has many opportunities every day to show our love toward God, neighbor, and self. Catholic Christians have a wonderful opportunity to practice love in many ways in the parish community, for it is in parish life that Catholic Christians live out their Catholic Faith and celebrate the milestones in the lives of those they love. Such milestones include Baptisms, Confirmations, First Communions, Funerals, Weddings, Quinceañeras, Presentations in the Church, and special anniversary blessings. Unfortunately, however, not everyone recognizes the treasure trove of opportunities that parish life has to offer. That is what the man in the following story learned from his pastor's visit.

There was once a parish priest who lived in a rural community. One day, he heard that one of his parishioners was going around telling people that he had decided not to go church anymore. The parishioner was telling his friends that he was able to communicate with God just as well on his own. After all, he reasoned, he could just as easily communicate with God in the fields and woods as he could in his parish church.

One winter evening, the parish priest went to the house of this rebellious parishioner for a friendly visit. The two men sat by the fireplace talking about things countrymen were interested in. Neither of them, however, brought up the issue church attendance or the lack of it. After some time talking, the priest casually took the fireplace tongs and grabbed a single coal from the fire. He placed the red-hot ember on the hearth.

The two men watched the isolated coal cease to burn and turn ashen gray while the other coals in the fireplace continued to burn brightly. The parish priest was silent. The wayward parishioner said, "I'll be at Mass next Sunday."

This wonderful story is very much in harmony with the Scripture messages of today, for it reminds us of the power of the community in our faith life. Here are three things we can learn about the importance of parish.

First, all Catholic Christians are called to be members of a parish community. To be a member of a parish, one must be formally registered. The parish is where Catholic Christians live out their faith in community. It is within the parish that we can formally worship and thank God for creating us and for all of our blessings. But also, the parish can be seen as a microcosm of the larger world. All the challenges and joys and dreams and hopes of the world are also present in parish life.

Second, the parish is our school of Christian living. Every week when we come to celebrate the Eucharist or Mass, we hear at least four Scripture passages. In these passages are important messages from God to us. Following the passages, the priest is then supposed to answer the question, "So, what? What do those Scripture passages have to do with me?" The priest tries to answer the "So, what?" question by means of a homily. He tries to make the words that were written many centuries ago come to life for the people of the community today. His homily may also contain a story that shows a practical application of the concepts the Scriptures were trying to get across to us.

Learning how to answer the "So, what?" question of the Scripture is very, very important, and every parent must do the same. All parents, by virtue of their baptism, are part of the "priesthood of all believers." As priests of the domestic church—their family—they are responsible for answering a child's questions about Scripture and faith. For example, it is one thing to tell children about the story of the Good Shepherd and the Lost Sheep, but it is another thing to be able to explain how the Good Shepherd is Jesus and how we are like lost sheep at times. When the shepherd brings us back from being lost, God is so happy that he throws a giant party in heaven with all the angels and saints because he loves us so much.

And third, the parish is a place where Catholic Christians get many opportunities to practice love by putting their faith into action. In our parish, for example, we serve God by serving others in many ways. We serve over nine thousand poor people in our social outreach ministry. We serve the poor in our St. Mary Health Center. We educate hundreds of children, youth, and adults in our five schools. We serve others in our missionary work on the Cape Fear Coast and in our sister parish in Honduras.

As we continue our life journey this week, it would be a good idea to take some time to explore how we treasure our parish and how we grow in it.

That is the good news I have for you on this Twenty-Third Sunday in Ordinary Time.

Story source: Anonymous, "In Community Is Strength," in Brian Cavanaugh's *The Sower's Seeds*, 1990, #90, p. 72.

Chapter 47

24th Sunday in Ordinary Time - A
Priest Forgives Killer

Scripture:

- Sirach 27: 30 – 28: 7
- Psalm 103: 1-2, 3-4, 9-10, 11-12
- Romans 14: 7-9
- Matthew 18: 21-35

As Catholic Christians come together to celebrate the Eucharist on this Twenty-Fourth Sunday in Ordinary Time, we hear powerful messages about the necessity of forgiveness in both the Old Testament and Gospel selections. We are called to imitate God, that is, to forgive others, as we want God to forgive us.

Oftentimes forgiving others is difficult. Each of us knows that when we reflect on the terrorist attacks that rocked our nation on September 11, 2001 when planes crashed into buildings in Washington and New York. Because forgiving others is often so difficult, it is always good to hear stories about how others chose to forgive rather than to be destroyed by hate. That is the theme in the following story by Warren Miller.

The story takes place in Grass Valley, California in the foothills of the Sierra Nevada Mountains. A winter storm from Alaska was bringing lots of cold rain and heavy flooding to the California community. Fr. O'Malley was sitting in his rectory writing his homily by candlelight. Suddenly, the phone rang. It was the hospital, asking if he would come to give "last rites" to a dying man.

Fr. O'Malley drove through the terrible storm and arrived at the hospital around 3:30 in the morning. He went to celebrate the Sacrament of the Sick with a man named Tom. Tom told Fr. O'Malley that when he was a young man, he did something so terrible that he had never told anyone about it. He also said that what he did was so bad that he hadn't spent a single day of his life without thinking about it and reliving the horror.

With Fr. O'Malley's prompting, Tom told his story. He said that it had been two nights before Christmas, and he had been working for the railroad. It was his job to push the switch for the tracks for oncoming trains. That night, he and his fellow crewmembers got drunk. Unfortunately, because he was drunk, he pushed the switch in the wrong direction for an oncoming train. Because of this, the train slammed into a car at the next crossing, killing a young man, his wife, and their two daughters.

Tom said "I have had to live with my being the cause of their deaths every day since then." Tom had never forgiven himself.

Fr. O'Malley was silent for a long moment. Then, he gently put his hand on Tom's shoulder and said very quietly, "If I can forgive you, God can forgive you, because in that car were my mother, my father, and my two sisters."

This story reminds us how powerful and noble forgiveness can be. And that is the theme of today's Scriptures.

For Christians, forgiveness is a critical virtue for Jesus commands it. Forgiveness is the act of being restored to a good relationship with God, others, and self, following a period or incident of sin or alienation. In the Christian tradition, forgiveness is accepting the unconditional mercy of God through Jesus and then extending that experience to other persons.

Forgiveness is a broad topic, but here are just three points that are good to know.

First, forgiveness is a cognitive thing, not always an affective thing. That means that to forgive, we use our heads, not our emotions. To forgive is a deliberate act of the will, whether we feel like it or not. Therefore, if we say we forgive another, we forgive them. If we begin to have feelings of resentments towards that other person, we must remind ourselves that we have forgiven them. When this happens to me, I say to myself, "Well, I said I forgave that person. Did I or did I not mean it?" Obviously I like to think I meant it.

Now forgiveness is not always easy. Sometimes we are hurt so badly that we often go through a period where we don't forgive another. Sometimes we may say, "I will forgive that person one day, but right now I'm just too angry or hurt or resentful." In other words, there is often a time when our emotions are more powerful than our Christian call to forgiveness.

To forgive is not to forget. Forgiveness is a virtue; forgetting is a biochemical condition. St. Julian of Norwich actually said, "Forgive and always remember."

Second, we should forgive because it is a Christian commandment. That is what Jesus taught us to do. Now it is important to remember that we are called to forgive *people*, not actions. We don't forgive evil actions. We forgive people. Though this is a simple concept, many people don't get it. They can't imagine forgiving others because they mistakenly believe that to forgive a person means they treat the behavior as acceptable.

The Christian commandment to forgive refers also to us, not just to others. Many people often forget the third part of the triple love command to love God, neighbor, and our selves. To not forgive ourselves is just as wrong as not forgiving others.

And third, when we don't forgive, we only hurt ourselves. Harboring resentments against others does not hurt them, but it does hurt us. This spiritual cancer eats away in our insides and can have disastrous effects on our mental, spiritual, and physical wellbeing. Nelson Mandela said, "Holding a grudge is like drinking poison and expecting your enemy to die." Forgiving others can be thought of as a selfish act, in that it is more certain to benefit ourselves than the person forgiven.

As we continue our life journeys this week, it would be a good idea to ask ourselves if we have anyone we need to forgive, and that includes ourselves. How is our lack of forgiveness harming us spiritually, emotionally, or physically?

And that is the good news I have for you on this Twenty-Fourth Sunday in Ordinary Time.

Story source: Warren Miller, "There Are No Coincidences," in Canfield, Hansen, Aubery, and Mitchell (Eds.) *Chicken Soup for the Christian Soul,* 1997, pp. 6-10.

Chapter 48

25th Sunday in Ordinary Time - A
Felipe On the Cross

Scripture:

- Isaiah 55: 6-9
- Psalm 145: 2-3, 8-9, 17-18
- Philippians 1: 20c-24, 27a
- Matthew 20: 1-16a

As Catholic Christians come together to celebrate the Eucharist on this Twenty-Fifth Sunday in Ordinary Time, we hear from the prophet Isaiah. He reminds us that the way God thinks is different from how humans think and that God's ways are above our ways. It is good to be reminded of that, for often we incorrectly believe that human logic must be like God's mind. When we begin thinking like that, we find we make many mistakes. That is what happened to a man named Felipe.

There was once a man named Felipe who lived in Mexico. Felipe was very religious, and he loved to visit the Lord in his town's church. But he felt this was not enough; he wanted to do something very special for the Lord.

So, one day, while he was looking up at Jesus on the cross, Felipe came to a decision. He would give Jesus a day off from being on the cross. After all, Felipe decided, Jesus must be very tired and bored being on the cross day after day, week after week, and month after month. Therefore, Felipe asked Jesus if he could take his place on the cross for a day. Jesus said that it would be okay but only under one condition: Felipe could listen, but under no circumstances was he permitted to speak. Felipe agreed to this condition and took Jesus' place on the cross.

Shortly after taking Jesus' place on the cross, a rich man came into the church to pray. When he was finished, he forgot to take his bag of money with him. Felipe said nothing. After awhile, a poor man came in to pray. To his surprise and delight, he discovered the bag of money and, when he was done praying, took the bag of money with him.

A third man, a traveler who was getting ready to take a cruise later that day, came to the church to ask Jesus for a safe trip. As he was praying, the rich man returned and began to accuse the traveler of stealing his money. When the traveler denied it, the rich man began beating him up. At this great injustice, Felipe could no longer keep silent. From the cross, Felipe cried out: "You fool! Stop beating up this man! He did not steal your money!"

The rich man was so astonished at Felipe speaking from the cross that he stopped beating up the traveler. As a result, the traveler was able to escape and just barely catch his ship. Unfortunately, the ship sank and everyone aboard died.

When Jesus returned, he was very disturbed by Felipe's lack of silence. He told Felipe that the rich man had more than enough money, and that the poor man desperately needed the money to feed his starving family. Also, if Felipe had kept silent, the traveler would have missed the doomed ship and would still be alive today.

The moral of the story is clear: only God knows the whole story. We humans only know a small fraction.

A good example of how God's will is different from human knowledge, we only have to look at today's Gospel story.

In this story, a landowner hired some laborers at dawn to work in his vineyard. When he hired them, he agreed on a just daily wage. Around 9 in the morning, the landowner went out and hired more workers for the vineyard. He did this again at noon, at 3 p.m., and at 5 p.m. When it was evening, the landowner gathered all the people he had hired during the day. To everyone's surprise, he gave each worker exactly the same amount of money.

Needless to say, the people who had worked since dawn felt they should be paid more, for they had worked so many more hours than the others. And, from a human perspective, they were right. It was not fair for someone who only worked since 5 in the afternoon to be paid the same as someone who had been working since dawn.

The moral of the story, however, is not about human justice or labor relations. Rather, Jesus said that this story is about what the "kingdom of heaven" is like. The landowner is to be seen as God, and the workers in the vineyard are those of us called to work in the kingdom. Each one is treated equally in the kingdom no matter what time we arrived there.

In looking at the Catholic Church in the United States, for example, we might compare the people hired at dawn to the Irish immigrants. After a while, Catholic Bohemians and Italians and Germans and others joined them. Still later, people came from India as well as from Vietnam and other Asian countries. And now we have the 5 o'clock people, the immigrants from Mexico as well as from nations of Central and South America.

All these Catholic Christians are full Catholic Christians. All are members of the household of Christ and all are equal parts of his Body.

Thus, we learn that the moral of the story of the landowner who hired workers at different times of day yet treated all of them equally was not about unfairness. On the contrary, it was about a God whose generosity is so wildly outrageous that it defies human logic. In short, God loves each of us beyond our wildest dreams, and God loves each and every one of us equally. What an incredible God we have! And because we are to imitate God in our lives, we are called to do the same with every person we meet.

As we continue our life journey this week, it would be a good idea to reflect on how generous God is with us, and how we imitate this outlandish generosity in our own lives.

And that is the good news I have for you on this Twenty-Fifth Sunday in Ordinary Time.

Chapter 49

26th Sunday in Ordinary Time - A
Wranglers Versus Stranglers

Scripture:

- Ezekiel 18: 25-28
- Psalm 25: 4-5, 6-7, 8-9
- Philippians 2: 1-11
- Matthew 21: 28-32

As Catholic Christians come together to celebrate the Eucharist on this Twenty-Sixth Sunday in Ordinary Time, we hear a most amazing command from St. Paul to the Philippians. Paul says: "Do nothing out of selfishness or out of vainglory; rather, humbly regard others as more important than yourselves, each looking out not for his own interests, but also for those of others" (2: 3-4).

This one sentence contains enough material for an incredible number of homilies exploring such concepts as humility, pride, self-centeredness, selfishness, stewardship, charity, and others. Today I focus on the importance of helping others on their life journeys. At St. Mary Parish, we call this "serving God by serving others."

The importance of helping others on their life journeys is seen clearly in the following story by Ted Engstrom called "Wranglers versus Stranglers."

There was once a group of very talented young men at an American university with great literary talent. These young men were studying to be poets, novelists, essayists, and creative non-fiction writers. They were exceptionally able to put the English language into writing. Regularly, these young men met to read and critique each other's works.

Unfortunately, these young men were ruthless in their criticism of one another. They criticized even the tiniest imperfections in each other's writing. They thought that being tough would bring out the best work in one another. Their sessions became so heartless and brutal that this exclusive writers' group gave themselves the nickname "The Stranglers."

On the same university campus were several women who were also studying to become great writers. They determined to start a group of future writers comparable to the men's group. They nicknamed their group "The Wranglers." Like the men, they came together to share their writing with one another. However, unlike the men, their criticism of one another's work was much softer, more positive, and more encouraging. In fact, often it was not criticism at all. The young women praised every effort, even the feeblest attempt, at writing, and they always sought to find something good to say about the writing they read.

Twenty years later, the university's alumni affairs office decided to study the careers of its alumni, and made an amazing discovery. They found that there was a tremendous difference in the literary accomplishments of "The

Stranglers" versus "The Wranglers." Of all the bright young men who had been part of "The Stranglers," not one of them had made any significant literary accomplishment of any kind. But from "The Wranglers," six or more of the women had become successful writers, some gaining national reputations.

When the two groups were compared, researchers guessed that the talent in the two groups was probably the same. The level of education of the men and women in the two groups was also the same. What was different, however, was that while "The Wranglers" determined to nurture each other and give each other a boost, "The Stranglers" created an atmosphere of contention and self-doubt. "The Wranglers" highlighted the best in each other, while "The Stranglers" highlighted the worst in each other.

This story is a very powerful illustration of love over hate, positivity over negativity, nurturing over grinding down.

But how does St. Paul's advice of looking out for other's interest apply to us today?

First, Paul's lesson is in harmony with Jesus' model of leadership. Recall that when Jesus was trying to teach the apostles how to be leaders of the Church, he knelt down on the floor and washed their feet. In other words, he showed them that to be the leader, one must put others' interests ahead of their own. This topsy-turvy view of leadership was something that ran contrary to the typical view of his time. The apostles were used to leaders being overbearing and haughty. Jesus' plan, however, was exactly the opposite. He served God by serving others, and so should we.

Second, notice that St. Paul said we are to look out for others' interests "also." That means that while we are to serve others and help them on their life journeys, we are also to nurture our own journey. This is the virtue of prudence. For example, every major financial adviser today reminds American parents that while it is nice to help their children pay for college, they must first fully plan for their own retirement. They reason that while there are many ways to fund a college education, there is only one way to fund retirement. When one reaches old age, one can't go back and do one's work life over again.

And third, St. Paul reminds us that we are not to function because of selfishness or vainglory. Vainglory, a word not used much anymore, refers to excessive pride in one's own achievements or abilities. People who are confident in their own abilities are much more likely to help others on their life journeys. They are not threatened by others' successes. In fact, they rejoice in helping others achieve. That is what all Christians should strive to achieve.

As we continue our life journeys this week, it would be a good idea to reflect on how we help others on their life journeys while doing the best we can on our own journey.

And that is the good news I have for you on this Twenty-Sixth Sunday in Ordinary Time.

Story source: Ted Engstrom, "Wranglers vs. Stranglers," in Brian Cavanaugh's *Fresh Sower's Seeds: Third Planting*, 1994, #35, pp. 33-34.

Chapter 50

27th Sunday in Ordinary Time - A
The Bull in the Road

Scripture:

- Isaiah 5: 1-7
- Psalm 80: 9 & 12, 13-14, 15-16, 19-20
- Philippians 4: 6-9
- Matthew 21: 33-43

Today as Catholic Christians come together to celebrate the Eucharist on this Twenty-Seventh Sunday in Ordinary Time, we hear the following message from St. Paul in his letter to the Philippians:

> "Have no anxiety at all, but in everything, by prayer and petition, with thanksgiving, make your requests known to God. Then the peace of God that surpasses all understanding will guard your hearts and minds in Christ Jesus" (Philippians 4: 6-7).

Now the concept of "anxiety" is something that we often ignore when talking about our faith, but it is a very important concept. It is so important, in fact, that every time we come to celebrate the Eucharist, we hear the priest say, immediately after the Lord's Prayer, "...keep us free from sin and protect us from all anxiety..."

Unlike "fear" which has a known cause, "anxiety" refers to being apprehensive or worried about what might happen in the future. Both fear and anxiety can harm our journey through life, thus diminishing the quality of life. It is only by confronting our fears and anxieties that we can make progress in the spiritual and mental parts of our lives. That is what the woman in the following story by Ruth Dreyer found out, much to her amazement and happiness.

There was once a woman standing on a road. As the woman looked ahead, she saw a huge, mean-looking bull. Unfortunately, the bull was blocking her path. The woman realized that the only way she could possibly continue was to get past this huge obstacle. That made her very frightened, for she had no idea what the bull would do to her if she encountered it head-on. For a long, long time, the woman and the bull stared at one another from a distance. The woman, frozen in her tracks, prayed that the bull would go away, but it did not. It simply stared back at her. But from the back of her mind, the woman heard a little voice whisper to her, "Do whatever it is you have to do to continue along the journey."

So the woman decided to gather all the strength she had and take the bull by the horns. She knew that if she were ever going to continue walking down the road, she would have to accept whatever consequences resulted when she confronted the bull—good, bad, or indifferent. So, with all her courage, she marched right up to the bull, grabbed his horns and said, "All right, Mr. Bull. You've got to get out of my way or fight with me—which will it be?"

Well, a most amazing thing happened. The bull sat right down on the road, sighed, and said to the woman, "What took you so long getting here? I've been standing her waiting to offer you a ride. Hop on my back and show me where you want to go."

What the woman had thought would be an insurmountable obstacle actually turned out to be a great blessing instead. All that she needed was the courage to take the action to discover the blessing.

This is a wonderful story because it highlights so well what St. Paul was talking about, and it's also a great story because it so frequently applies to our own lives. Frequently we have anxieties and fears that can paralyze us, diminishing the qualities of our lives and the lives of those around us.

Here are just three points we can make about fears and anxieties in our lives.

First, we all have fears and anxieties from time to time. Some of them are okay, while others are not. For example, I am afraid of rattlesnakes. I don't know if I've ever seen one, but I am one-hundred percent positive that I would be terrified of one if I saw one outside of a container because I know they can kill people. I think this is a good fear because it would protect me from harm if I ever encountered a rattlesnake in real life.

Second, some fears and anxieties can harm us by affecting the quality of our lives. For example, some people have such a great fear of failure that they become paralyzed. They believe that by doing nothing, rather than doing something, they cannot fail. Likewise, people who fear rejection by others can go through life building emotional walls around themselves so that nobody can get too close to their hearts and spirits and harm them. Such fears and anxieties prevent a person from growing and experiencing life to the fullest. And that, my friends, is not what God had in mind for us when he created us.

And third, when we find ourselves confronted with fears and anxieties that are potentially harmful to our wellbeing, we can take measures to combat them. For example, we can follow Paul's advice and pray about these fears. Or we can try to imagine the worst possible scenario and realize that even in the worst case, we would survive. Or, we can engage in what I like to call the "Nike response." Nike, maker of tennis shoes, has a slogan called "Just do it." Often in my life, when faced with something I fear or have anxiety about, I say "Just do it" and then go ahead and "just do it." It works amazingly well!

As we continue our life journey this week, it would be a good idea to take some time to reflect on the fears and anxieties we have. Which are harmless and which are potentially harmful to the quality of our lives? How do we deal with these fears and anxieties?

And that is the good news I have for you on this Twenty-Seventh Sunday in Ordinary Time.

Story source: Ruth Dreyer, "The Day the Bull Stood in the Road (adapted)," in Brian Cavanaugh's *Fresh Packet of Sower's Seeds: Third Planting*, 1994, #84, pp. 76-77.

Chapter 51

28th Sunday in Ordinary Time - A
Detachment and Resiliency

Scripture:

- Isaiah 25: 6-10a
- Psalm 23: 1-3a, 3b-4, 5, 6
- Philippians 4: 12-14, 19-20
- Matthew 22: 1-14

Today as Catholic Christians come together to celebrate the Eucharist on this Twenty-Eighth Sunday in Ordinary Time, we hear the very interesting story of the king who gave a wedding feast for his son and invited many wedding guests. Unfortunately, though, the invited guests didn't show up. The king sent out a second invitation to the guests, but they still didn't come. Finally, the king sent his workers out into the streets to invite everyone they could find. When the newly invited guests arrived, the king noticed that one of them did not have on the correct wedding garment. He threw this man out of the wedding banquet hall.

Now for many years, this parable did not make any sense to me. After all, I reasoned, what kind of a no-good king would be so insensitive as to throw a guest out of a banquet because he didn't like the way he was dressed? After all, the king in this story represents God. But then, in the seminary, I learned a piece of information that made the story finally make sense. What I learned was that in the time of Jesus, it was the responsibility of the wedding <u>host</u> to provide proper wedding garments to anyone who did not have one. So if a person showed up at the banquet table improperly dressed, it meant that he or she deliberately refused to put on the proper garment given by the host. Now the story made sense.

In this parable, God is the one giving the banquet, and Jesus is the Son. We are the guests, for we are all invited to the banquet. The banquet could refer to heaven or the Kingdom of God or the Eucharist. It doesn't matter. What is important in this story is that we are invited and we are to be properly dressed.

Being "properly dressed" in this context, however, has absolutely nothing to do with our clothing. The "garment" we are to wear refers to clothing ourselves in Christian virtues. In other words, we are to live our lives in a virtuous way.

In today's letter of St. Paul to the Philippians, for example, we can see two of the virtues that Paul demonstrated in his life: detachment and resiliency. Though the virtues are different, they often travel together in daily life.

Detachment is sometimes referred to as being *"in* the world but not *of* the world." In other words, we can own possessions without letting them own us. If we lose material things, we don't go to pieces. Detachment leads to other virtues such as serenity and generosity.

Resiliency refers to bouncing back after one is knocked down. When I was growing up, there was an inflatable toy called a "Joe Palooka." Kids could continually punch Joe Palooka, but he would always bounce back up; he could never "stay down."

In Paul's letter, he noted that he knew how to live in humble circumstances and how to live in abundance. He knew how to be hungry and how to be satisfied. No matter what life threw at him, he kept his eyes on serving God through the grace of Jesus. He was detached as all missionaries are called to be. Missionaries can thoroughly enjoy a steak dinner in the United States while on vacation, but they can be just as satisfied with beans and water in a poor mission country. Externals don't matter that much to the true missionary. And people who are resilient always bounce back. In the United States, we have an expression about resiliency that says, "You can't keep a good man down." St. Paul was like that.

In many years of nursing, I have had the privilege of witnessing detachment and resiliency close up. In the following story, we see both of these virtues in action.

The story comes from a large state mental hospital in Oklahoma. I was supervising nursing students in several wards. One ward was particularly depressing. It contained rows upon rows of beds in a large dormitory, and for the most part, the men on the ward simply sat all day long on their beds, staring at the floor. Some of this behavior was undoubtedly due to the medication they were on, while some of the behavior was due to severe depression and other forms of mental illness.

One young man, however, was markedly different from all the other men. For this young man, whom I'll call Terry, there were not enough hours in the day to do all the things he wanted to do. He loved to take walks on the campus and talk with those he met. He loved to visit the canteen to see what new items the store had gotten in. He loved to visit the patients' library, check out books, and spend hours reading. He loved to attend the movies the hospital had on occasion, he enjoyed the occasional BINGO games and dances the hospital had from time to time, and he loved to play volleyball.

Terry was a poster boy for detachment and resiliency. Though he was in a dismal place, he seemed not to notice the negatives all around him. Rather, he only saw the exciting opportunities that were present. He never lost hope, and he never lost joy. He was glad to be part of the universe, and every day he woke up wondering what wonderful things he would experience that day.

As we continue our life journeys this week, it would be a good idea to reflect a bit on the virtues of detachment and resiliency. Do we own our possessions, or do they own us? Do we bounce back from the trials of life, or do we let life problems conquer us?

And that is the good news I have for you on this Twenty-Eighth Sunday in Ordinary Time.

Chapter 52

29th Sunday in Ordinary Time - A
Generosity and the Heart of Gold

Scripture:

- Isaiah 45: 1, 4-6
- Psalm 96: 1 & 3, 4-5, 7-8, 9-10a & c
- 1 Thessalonians 1: 1-5b
- Matthew 22: 15-21

As Catholic Christians come to celebrate the Eucharist on this Twenty-Ninth Sunday in Ordinary Time, we hear the story of the Pharisees who were trying to trap Jesus by his speech.

To do this, they asked Jesus if it was lawful to pay census taxes to Caesar. They figured that no matter which way Jesus answered, they could condemn him. Jesus, however, knew the malice they had in their hearts. So he took a coin and asked them whose image was on the coin. When they answered, "Caesar's," he said, "Then repay to Caesar what belongs to Caesar and to God what belongs to God" (Matthew 22: 21).

Now this teaching of Jesus is just one part of Jesus' larger message about things of the Earth. Today's lesson illustrates two parts of the larger message: (1) we really don't "own" material things because when we leave this world, there is not one single material thing we can take with us; and (2) we are called to be good stewards of the material world, and that includes sharing abundantly with others.

The man in the following story by Florence Myles understood very well what Jesus was teaching. The story is called "Heart of Gold."

It was Thanksgiving, a day when Americans thank God for the many blessings that he has showered upon them. It is also the time when Americans celebrate by eating a lot of food, especially turkey and all the trimmings. But in one house, there was no delicious smell of turkey roasting in the oven, no pies cooling on the counter, and no beautiful table setting. The mother had lost her job a few weeks earlier. Her daughter's tiny salary went to pay the rent. A son was still in school, and there was no father in the home. Things looked very bleak this Thanksgiving. The mother was cooking some leftover stew on the stove and warming up some day-old bread in the oven. She was a proud woman and didn't want anyone to know how bad things were in her home.

Suddenly there was a knock at the door. When she opened it, there was Mr. Gold, a door-to-door salesman who kept everyone supplied with things for their houses. He stood there with his arms full of grocery bags and a smile on his face. "May I come begging to you today?" he asked. "Here it is Thanksgiving Day, and I have no place to go and no one to share it with."

The mother was embarrassed, but she invited him in and started to explain that they didn't have much to eat on this special day. But before she could continue, Mr. Gold, who knew quite well that the family was having serious financial trouble, interrupted her by saying, "Here, I have all this food. It's only chicken, but who's to know?" He then began unpacking the groceries. There was enough food for a great feast, from soup to nuts, plus two pies for dessert.

The family had a wonderful Thanksgiving feast that year. Mr. Gold didn't eat too much, but nobody seemed to notice. When he was leaving, he thanked the family for taking such good care of a lonely old man on that Thanksgiving Day.

This story is an excellent example of the teaching of Jesus about the material world. Let's look at the two principles that Jesus taught in his response to the Pharisees about paying a census tax to the government.

First, although we often use the word "own" to refer to things of this world, we really own nothing material. Rather, we simply "handle" the things of the physical world until we die. Then these things are either discarded or handled by someone else. Let's take money for example. For many decades now, most Americans have not received a physical paycheck. Rather, our earnings are deposited directly into our checking accounts. We then spend the money by moving it from one place to another. Some we give to the electric company, and some we give to the grocery store. Some we give to the gas station, while other money we give as Christmas or birthday gifts. Some we invest for our retirement or use to buy houses and cars and clothes and whatever. When it's time to leave this Earth for heaven, our money and all it bought will be left wherever we have scattered it. This is an amazing concept!

The second major principle that Jesus taught us about money and material things is that we are to be good stewards. The principles of stewardship that Jesus taught can be summarized in four statements.

First, all good things come from God. These gifts include family, friends, and material goods, and they include such abstractions as our desire for hard work, opportunities, dreams, and other intangibles.

Second, we are called to care for and develop our gifts. In this country, for example, we place a high value on developing our brains by formal education.

Third, we are to share our gifts with others, and we are to share them abundantly. Jesus taught this principle frequently. He also promised that the more generous we are, the more generous God will be with us.

And finally, we are to give to God the "first fruits" of our labor. "First fruits" means "off the top," the first ten percent of our bounty goes to the Lord.

As we continue our life journeys this week, it would be a good idea to take some time to reflect on the principles Jesus was teaching us in his talk with the Pharisees. Do we understand that there is nothing in the material world that we can take with us to eternity? Are we good and generous stewards of what God has entrusted to us?

And that is the good news I have for you on this Twenty-Ninth Sunday in Ordinary Time.

Story source: Florence Myles, "Heart of Gold," in Brian Cavanaugh's *Sower's Seeds That Nurture Family Values: Sixth Planting,* 2000, #39, p. 49.

Chapter 53

30ᵗʰ Sunday in Ordinary Time - A
Bl. Clemente Vismara, PIME

Scripture:

- Exodus 22: 20-26
- Psalm 18: 2-3a, 3bc-4, 47 & 51ab
- 1 Thessalonians 1: 5c-10
- Matthew 22: 34-40

Today as we come together to celebrate the Thirtieth Sunday in Ordinary Time, Catholic Christians throughout the world celebrate World Mission Sunday. This is a day when we are reminded that every one of us, because of our baptism, is called to share Christ with others. But on World Mission Sunday, we especially remember that we are called to support those who give their lives serving on the front lines in poor parts of the world.

In our country, Catholics get into their cars and drive to church each weekend. When they arrive at church, they expect an ordained priest to greet them, celebrate the Eucharist, and give them Holy Communion. Following Mass, they drive back home. The whole experience will take less than two hours for most Catholics in the United States.

But in many parts of the world, this scenario cannot take place. In many parts of the world, as in our sister parish in Honduras, people do not have cars. And even if they did have cars, the primitive "roads" are sometimes impassable. Right now in our sister parish, for example, our two priests cannot get to many of their 87 churches and chapels because of massive flooding, and two of their 87 churches and chapels have been destroyed by the floods. In many poor parts of the world, people walk for hours just to get to a church; that is the case in our sister parish. And in many parts of the world, even if people could get to church, there are no ordained priests for them.

Because of this reality, Catholic Christians on World Mission Sunday not only recognize that they are responsible for supporting our missionaries who work on the front-lines with our prayers and financial support, but we also honor those who give their lives in this special way. Today I would like to introduce you a very remarkable man by the name of Clemente Vismara, sometimes known as "The Man Who Never Grew Old."

Clemente was born in Milan, Italy in 1897. His father was a saddler, and his mother was a seamstress. After being orphaned, he was raised by relatives.

As a young man he served in World War I and was honorably discharged in 1919 with the rank of Sergeant Major. He received three medals for bravery.

Clemente was ordained in 1926 as part of the Pontifical Institute for Foreign Missions—PIME, which is the abbreviation of the Latin name. Fr. Clemente was then sent to Burma, which today is also known as

Myanmar. Fr. Clemente was noted for his amazing energy. He went into primitive areas of Burma and devoted much of his time to improving the lives of the people. For example, in Burmese society in that time, women were often abused, abandoned or sold. Many men were jobless and often addicted to opium. Fr. Clemente went to work to correct this.

Fr. Clemente helped the men learn trades by becoming farmers, tailors, barbers, lumberjacks, and masons. But his main focus was to help women and children, orphans and widows. From the very beginning, Fr. Clemente was known as the "Apostle of the Little Ones."

Fr. Clemente opened orphanages, founded factories, built parishes, founded schools, taught carpentry and mechanics, built brick houses, planted rice fields, made irrigation canals, and introduced the people to crops they had never had before, such as wheat, corn, and different kinds of vegetables. By helping the people raise their standard of living, they were able to listen to the Word of God that Fr. Clemente preached. Today in Burma, many people are named Clement and Clementina.

In 1988, Fr. Clemente died, and on June 26, 2011, Pope Benedict XVI declared Clemente to be Blessed Clemente Vismara, the last step in the process towards being named a Saint of the Catholic Church.

Blessed Clemente was a man who loved his vocation. He always remarked that he could not help but be a joyful person, for God had blessed him with a wonderful family, his Catholic Christian faith, a vocation as a missionary priest, and a purpose in life. Many people who have studied his life say that Blessed Clemente thrived on serving others. In fact, Clemente himself wrote that one only grows old when he no longer has something productive to give. Because he spent his whole life serving God by serving others, he became known as "The Man Who Never Grew Old." At age ninety-one, Fr. Clemente was just as enthusiastic about his vocation as a priest and a missionary as he was when he was first ordained.

When we look at the life of Blessed Clemente Vismara, we see a man totally in love with God, a man whose only way of showing this love was serving others. That is what kept him forever young in his heart and spirit. The "secret" of staying young is not found in an operating room or in magic elixirs or pills or face creams. It is in having a passion for serving God by serving others. It is in being passionate about a cause.

As we continue our life journey this week, it would be a good idea to examine our own lives. How do we serve God by serving others? How do we reflect the missionary spirit in our lives?

And that is the good news I have for you on this Thirtieth Sunday in Ordinary Time.

___

Story sources:

- Gheddo, Piero. "Fr. Clemente Vismara: Patriarch of Burma to be declared blessed. AsiaNews.It, May 10, 2011.
- Blessed Clement Vismara – PIME Video.

Chapter 54

31st Sunday in Ordinary Time - A
The Humble Abbot

Scripture:

- Malachi 1: 14b – 2: 2b, 8-10
- Psalm 131: 1, 2, 3
- 1 Thessalonians 2: 7b-9, 13
- Matthew 23: 1-12

As Catholic Christians come to celebrate the Eucharist on this Thirty-First Sunday in Ordinary Time, we hear Jesus talk about the humility that a church leader should possess. In the United States, this Sunday is also known as "Priesthood Sunday."

Priesthood Sunday was started in 2003 as a response to the scandals that were occurring in the ordained priesthood. The purpose of Priesthood Sunday is to honor the ordained priesthood and show support for the vast majority of priests in this country who live their vocations faithfully.

Though all Christians become part of the "priesthood of all believers" at their Baptism when the Holy Spirit enters into them, Priesthood Sunday honors ordained priests and bishops. In this homily, I will use the word "priest" to refer to ordained priests, in particular those who work in parishes.

In the Gospel reading of today, Jesus is condemning the behaviors of the Scribes and Pharisees of his day. Instead of being humble in their ministry, they were proud and arrogant. They laid heavy burdens on the people, but they themselves did not follow what they preached. They sought honors and status. In today's world, there are unfortunately religious leaders like that, even in the Catholic Church. These are people who live what I call the "imperial priesthood," a priesthood that is the exact opposite of the servant leadership model Jesus wanted his disciples to follow.

In the following story by William Barclay, we learn of a wonderful priest who did follow Jesus' example of servant-leadership.

Once there was a holy priest monk who was a simple, humble man. One day, his superiors told him that he was to become the abbot, or head monk, of a distant monastery. Being very obedient, he packed up his few belongings and traveled to the new monastery, which he had never seen before. The new abbot arrived unannounced at the new place. The monks of the monastery looked him over and decided he was very unimpressive because of his simple appearance. Before the new abbot could introduce himself, the monks ordered him to work in the kitchen at very menial tasks. Being a humble and obedient man, the new abbot immediately went to work, spending long hours washing the floors, cleaning dishes, shelling beans, preparing food, and scrubbing pots and pans. This went on for some days.

After a week or so, the bishop of the diocese where the monastery was located came to see how the new abbot was doing. When the monks told the bishop that the new abbot had never shown up, the bishop went searching for him. To his amazement, he found the new abbot busy preparing that evening's dinner.

That evening, when all the monks were gathered in the chapel for Evening Prayer, the bishop officially presented the new abbot to the monks. The monks received a lesson in humility that they never forgot.

On this Priesthood Sunday, it is good to reflect on the priesthood, for without ordained priests, we could not have the Eucharist or Mass. Without Mass, we would lose the "source and summit" of our spirituality. Here are three points worth considering about ordained priests.

First, parish priests are called to preach the word of God, celebrate sacraments with the people, and be the leaders of a parish community. To prepare for these tasks, men go to school a minimum of eight years following high school, but usually much longer.

Some parish priests are pastors, like me. The role of pastor includes not only all the ministerial duties that a priest has, but also administrative things like creating budgets, hiring staff, setting a vision for the future, caring for the physical plant, adopting sister parishes, and a myriad of other tasks. While seminaries prepare men to be priests, they rarely prepare them with the skill sets to be pastors. Never, for example, did I learn about budgets or fundraising in the seminary.

Second, the priesthood is filled with joys and challenges, and God showers priests with special graces to function well. But that is true in any vocation, isn't it? God showers parents with the graces needed to be good and faithful parents.

Sometimes people talk about the "sacrifices" that ordained priests must make. From my perspective, however, parents are called to make many more "sacrifices" in their vocations than priests are ever called to make. I believe that if you are in the vocation God has called you to, and are living it to the best of your ability, you will be filled with joy. I find that every day of being a priest is a total joy, even on days when challenges seem insurmountable. I know that people who are called to be parents or single persons would say the same thing about their vocations.

And third, priests make mistakes both as priests and as pastors. This is no news to any of us. Like people in any vocation, we are called to grow and flourish. Like Jesus, who fell on the way to Calvary, priests - and anyone for that matter - should learn from mistakes and make every effort to avoid them in the future. For anyone whom I may have hurt as a priest or pastor in the past, please accept my sincerest apology.

As we continue our life journey this week, it would be a good idea to take some time to reflect on the ordained priesthood. What qualities do you think make a good priest?

That is the good news I have for you on this Thirty-First Sunday in Ordinary Time.

Story source: "Hypocrisy of the Pharisees," in Gerard Fuller's *Stories for All Seasons for Every Sunday, Every Year, Every Preacher, Every Teacher,* 1997, p. 43. William Barclay, quoted by James Gilhooley, *Pastoral Life* (43): 57, 31st Sunday OT, Year A, Oct., 1993.

Chapter 55

32nd Sunday in Ordinary Time – A
Special Message to Deliver

Scripture:

- Wisdom 6: 12-16
- Psalm 63: 2, 3-4, 5-6, 7-8
- 1 Thessalonians 4: 13-18
- Matthew 25: 1-13

Today as Catholic Christians gather to celebrate the Eucharist, they hear Jesus' story about the ten virgins who were waiting for their master to return home. Five of the virgins were wise, and five were foolish. The wise ones prepared for an unknown hour when the master would return by ensuring that they had plenty of oil in their lamps. The foolish ones, though, did not plan. Because they didn't plan, they ran out of oil. When the master returned, the foolish virgins were unprepared.

This parable reminds us that we are to always be prepared for the Lord when he comes for us at the end of our lives here on Earth. Jesus tells us, "...stay awake, for you know neither the day nor the hour" (Matthew 25: 13). It is fitting that this parable comes to us on this Thirty-Second Sunday in Ordinary Time, for the end of the current church year is only three weeks away. And just as the church year will surely come to an end, so eventually will our lives.

The question that this parable raises for us is how we are to be ready for the Lord when he comes to take us to heaven. Certainly one of the main ways to be ready is to live our lives abundantly every day. That means that we are to embrace life and to live it to the fullest. We are to cherish our vocations and do our best every day.

As our lives progress, what we are called to do changes depending on our circumstances. For example, a schoolgirl's vocation is very different from what she will be called to do as a mother, and what she will be called to do as a grandmother will be still different. But regardless of what we are called to do at any given point in our life, we are called to do the best we can. That is what the anonymous writer shows us in the following essay, called "You have a special message to deliver."

> There is an old Jewish-Christian tradition which says:
> God sends each person into this world
> with a special message to deliver,
> with a special song to sing for others,
> with an act of love to bestow.
>
> No one else can speak my message,
> or sing my song, or offer my act of love.

These are entrusted only to me.
According to this tradition,
the message may be spoken,
the song sung, the act of love delivered
only to a few, or to all the folk in a small town,
or to all the people in a large city,
or even to all those in the whole world.

It all depends on God's unique plan for each person.
To which we might add:
The greatest gift of God, one would think,
is the gift of life.
The greatest sin of humans, it would seem,
would be to return that gift,
ungrateful and unopened.

I love this piece because it reminds us that life is God's gift to us, and what we make of our life is our gift to God. Not only that, but it reminds us that every single human is unique, and each of us has something unique to give to the world.

To fully appreciate our life and how we are to live it, it would be good to reflect on the four parts of good stewardship.

First, we realize that our life is a gift from God, so we need to thank God from whom all gifts flow.

Second, we need to take the gift of our life and develop it as much as we can. That means we need to develop our minds and bodies through proper nutrition, exercise, and education. It means that we try to make something of ourselves rather than sitting around vegetating and simply taking up space in the environment.

When we have developed our selves, we are then called to abundantly share ourselves with others. In other words, we are to follow Jesus' command to help those in need all around us. We do this through our vocations as Christians, as well as through our specific occupations and interests.

Finally, we are to give the "first fruits" of our labor to God. That means that we put God ahead of all else.

As we continue our life journey this week, it would be a good idea to take stock of our own lives. How do we our life to the fullest? In what areas of our lives do we need to change so we can flourish? What unique message do we have for the world to hear?

And that is the good news I have for you on this Thirty-Second Sunday in Ordinary Time.

Story source: Anonymous, "You Have a Special Message to Deliver," in Brian Cavanaugh's *Sower's Seeds Aplenty: Fourth Planting,* 1996, #43, pp. 32-33.

Chapter 56

33rd Sunday in Ordinary Time - A
The Talent of Grandma Moses

Scripture:

- Proverbs 31: 10-13, 19-20, 30-31
- Psalm 128: 1-2, 3, 4-5
- 1 Thessalonians 5: 1-6
- Matthew 25: 14-30

Today as Catholic Christians gather to celebrate the Eucharist on this Thirty-Third Sunday in Ordinary Time, we hear Jesus' wonderful parable of the talents.

In the parable, a man was going on a journey, so he entrusted his servants with different amounts of money to take care of while he was gone. A "talent," in Jesus' time, was a lot of money, worth about 20 years of wages for a common worker. The master gave each servant a different number of talents depending on the servant's abilities. One he gave five talents, another two, and the third he gave one talent. After he had been away for a long time, he returned. He was delighted to learn that the one who had been given five talents had doubled his money. The one who had been given two had also doubled his money. The master was so impressed with the ingenuity and resourcefulness of the two servants, that he increased their responsibilities. The third servant, however, had buried his single talent and, therefore, had produced nothing. The master was very unhappy with him.

Now the moral of this story is not that we should become financially richer, although there is nothing wrong with being rich as long as we are generous. Rather, the moral of the story is that we should take the gifts that God gives us and develop them. That means that we are to grow and flourish, never stagnate. As long as we have life, we should be changing in a positive direction. This is a basic principle of Christian stewardship.

Some people, however, are lazy. They are content to be mediocre in their approach to life. Others get into a rut in their lives from which they never get out. Others think that perhaps they are too old to grow, that growth is something only for children and youth. But all Christians are called to grow spiritually, and this includes, from my perspective, both our intellect and our mental health.

A very inspirational example of a woman who developed her talents when she was over seventy years old is "Grandma Moses," an American folk artist extraordinaire.

Anna Mary Robertson was born on a farm in 1860 in Greenwich, New York, one of ten children.

When she was twenty-seven, Anna married a hired hand by the name of Thomas Salmon Moses. Thomas and Anna went to live on a farm in Virginia and had ten children, five of whom died in birth. In 1905, the couple went to live in Eagle Bridge, New York. Thomas died in 1927, but Anna continued to farm with the help of one of her sons.

Anna, in addition to being a mother and farmer, loved to "make something from nothing." For example, she could take scraps of cloth and turn them into beautiful quilts. She loved to embroider, but she had to abandon that when she developed arthritis.

When she was in her seventies, Anna began to paint. She told reporters that she began to paint when she wanted to make the postman a Christmas gift. Anna said that painting was easier than baking a cake over a hot stove. Anna's art was known as primitive art, and she liked to give her pieces to family and friends. Over thirty years, she produced over 3,600 canvas paintings.

In 1938, a New York art collector saw her little paintings displayed in a drug store, priced from $3 to $5. The collector bought all the paintings and went to visit Anna. The following year, three of Anna's paintings were included in "Contemporary Unknown American Painters" at the Museum of Modern Art in New York City. This soon led to her own showing, called "What a Farm Wife Painted."

Soon Anna began to be called "Grandma Moses," and art collectors from all over the world clamored to get one of her paintings. Soon her paintings were found on Christmas cards and tiles and fabrics not only in the United States, but all over the world. Her 1943 painting called "Sugaring Off" sold for $1.2 million.

Grandma Moses, who always insisted that she was much prouder of her preserves and family than she was of her paintings, received many honors in her life from Presidents, universities, magazines, and other sources.

Grandma Moses died in December of 1961 when she was 101 years old.

The story of Grandma Moses is truly inspirational. It is especially wonderful to know that some of the best and most creative years can be when we are older. Today, of course, that is even truer than it was in Grandma Moses' time, as we live longer and healthier than ever before.

Probably none of us will ever achieve the fame of Grandma Moses. That is okay. All of us are, however, called to grow and flourish as people. All of us are called to approach this life filled with wonder and dreams and enthusiasm. All of us are called to use the gifts that God gave us and develop them as Grandma Moses did. And, as Christians, we are then called to share these gifts with others, especially those who have little.

As we continue our life journeys this week, it would be a good idea to stop and reflect on how we are growing as people. How do we use the talents that God gave us? How do we share them with others?

And that is the good news I have for you on this Thirty-Third Sunday in Ordinary Time.

Information about Grandma Moses was obtained from *Wikipedia,* 2011.

Chapter 57

Christ the King - A
St. Martin of Tours

Scripture:

- Ezekiel 34: 11-12, 15-17
- Psalm 23: 1-2a, 2b-3, 5-6
- 1 Corinthians 15: 20-26, 28
- Matthew 25: 31-46

This Sunday, Catholic Christians celebrate the final Sunday of the church year with the Feast of Christ the King. This past year we have heard the life of Jesus mostly from the Gospel of Matthew. Next week, as we begin a new church year, we'll hear mostly from the Gospel of Mark.

On this feast day, we catch a glimpse of the final judgment. Jesus, the eternal king, will judge the nations. In this story, Jesus will separate the good from the bad. The good are those who practiced the works of mercy towards their fellow human beings. That means they recognized Jesus in every person and then acted on the basis of this recognition. The bad, on the other hand, did not recognize Jesus in people who needed help, so they failed to act in a charitable way.

Though there are many stories of people serving Christ by serving others, one of my favorite stories comes from a most remarkable man who lived in the fourth century, St. Martin of Tours.

Martin was born in what is now the country of Hungary around 315. Martin's father was a Roman army officer. Martin's parents were not Christians.

When he was only ten years old, Martin became a Catholic Christian catechumen, a person desiring to become baptized. When he was fifteen, he was forced into the Roman army and entered the cavalry. Like his father, he eventually became an officer assigned to France.

Even as an army officer, though, Martin led the life of a monk. For example, instead of having a servant polish his boots, he insisted on polishing the boots of his servant.

One of the most famous stories about Martin occurred when he was an Army officer and still a catechumen. One bitterly cold day in winter, as Martin was riding through the gates of a town, he saw a beggar sitting on the side of the road. The beggar's clothes were ragged, and he was freezing. Martin, filled with compassion, stopped, got off his horse, took off his beautiful tunic, and slashed the tunic in half. He gave one half of the tunic to the freezing beggar to wrap himself in. Many who witnessed this amazing spectacle jeered Martin, but some in the crowd recognized that they were witnessing Christian goodness.

Later that night, as Martin slept, he had a dream. In the dream he saw Jesus wearing the half mantle that he had given the beggar. Jesus told all the saints and angels around him, "See! This is the mantle that Martin, yet a catechumen, gave me." When Martin awoke in the morning, he immediately went to be baptized.

Now in those days, one could not be a Christian and a soldier at the same time, so Martin had to renounce his military position. Though his superiors were very much against this, Martin eventually got his way.

Eventually Martin found himself in Poitiers and made friends with St. Hilary. Martin devoted himself to prayer and preached against the Arian heresy, as did Hilary. Martin spent much time in a hermitage in the wilderness, and then founded a monastery. There men came to seek him out for spiritual direction.

One day, the Bishop of Tours died, and the people needed a new bishop. In those days the people chose bishops. Because everyone knew of Martin's holiness, they devised a trick to get him to become bishop. A resident of Tours went to visit Martin and begged him to visit his sick wife. When Martin arrived in the city, the villagers surrounded him so he could not get away. The people insisted that Martin become their bishop, but the other local bishops took one look at the dirty, ragged, and disheveled appearance of Martin, and decided to oppose that move. The people, however, declared that they didn't choose Martin because of his haircut, but because of his holiness and poverty. Overwhelmed by the crowds, the bishops ordained Martin as bishop. Martin lived a very simple and holy life as a bishop, with a special love for those on the margins of society, especially prisoners.

The story of Martin is inspirational in itself. It is very relevant also to today's Gospel story of Christ the King judging the nations. The judging will be on works of mercy, according to this story.

Corporal Works of Mercy are actions to fulfill the physical needs of others. The word "corporal" comes from the Latin word meaning "body." The Corporal Works of Mercy are seven: to feed the hungry, give drink to the thirsty, clothe the naked, visit the imprisoned, shelter the homeless, visit the sick, and bury the dead.

Spiritual Works of Mercy are charitable actions to help those with spiritual and emotional needs. The Spiritual Works of Mercy are to admonish the sinner, instruct the ignorant, counsel the doubtful, comfort the sorrowful, bear wrongs patiently, forgive all injuries, and pray for the living and the dead.

When we engage in the works of mercy, we are putting our faith into action. We are not simply "talking the talk," but, rather, we're "walking the walk." According to Jesus, we will be judged on the basis of how we put our faith into action.

As we continue our life journey this week, it would be a good idea to ask ourselves how we practice the Corporal and Spiritual Works of Mercy.

And that is the good news I have for you on this final Sunday of the Church Year, the Feast of Christ the King.

Story source: "St. Martin of Tours," in *Butler's Lives of the Saints: November — New Full Edition,* Revised by Sarah Fawcett Thomas, 1997, Collegeville, Minnesota, Burns & Oates, The Liturgical Press, pp. 83-87.

Made in the USA
San Bernardino, CA
20 August 2016